Once there Was a Place Called Sampson

Once there Was a Place Called Sampson

Latrell Pappy Mickler

Copyright © 2009 by Latrell Pappy Mickler

All rights reserved. No part of this book shall be reproduced or transmitted in any form or by any means, electronic, mechanical, magnetic, photographic including photocopying, recording or by any information storage and retrieval system, without prior written permission of the publisher. No patent liability is assumed with respect to the use of the information contained herein. Although every precaution has been taken in the preparation of this book, the publisher and author assume no responsibility for errors or omissions. Neither is any liability assumed for damages resulting from the use of the information contained herein.

ISBN 978-0-7414-5568-0

Published by:

INFINITY PUBLISHING
1094 New DeHaven Street, Suite 100
West Conshohocken, PA 19428-2713
Info@buybooksontheweb.com
www.buybooksontheweb.com
Toll-free (877) BUY BOOK
Local Phone (610) 941-9999
Fax (610) 941-9959

Printed in the United States of America

Published March 2013

Dedicated to the memory
of Sampson's pioneers
and to their descendants.

Contents

Introduction	- 1 -
Sampson	- 3 -
The Minorcans: They Came, They Suffered, They Conquered	- 57 -
When German-Dutch Protestants Met Minorcan Catholics	- 65 -
Some Early Pioneers and the Loretto Parish	- 69 -
Confederate Scout William A. Mickler	- 73 -
One Heroic Catholic Family	- 85 -
Bobwhite Quail Hunting: Not what it Used to Be	- 89 -
Daddy's Bargain	- 93 -
Mullet on the Beach!	- 101 -
Gopher Stew	- 107 -
Monsignor Dawson Remembers St. Joseph's	- 113 -
Sinister Insects: First Aid Afield	- 117 -
Poisonous Mouth of the River	- 127 -
Maynard H. Cox, Snakebite Specialist	- 139 -
The Gulf	- 147 -
Call of the Gobbler	- 153 -
Why Not Bring *Two Loves* Together?	- 157 -
Tom Meets the Temptress	- 163 -
How to Count Turkeys	- 169 -
Believe it or *Not!*	- 175 -
Acknowledgments	- 179 -

Introduction

Once there Was a Place Called Sampson is a collection of stories, some previously published, some new, and all Florida related. The first is a about the place where I was raised and which has lost its identity due in part to all the new subdivisions in the once rural area. Other stories are from my childhood in the 1940's and '50s. Still others are historical, nostalgic, or informative. All of the stories are true and indicative of my life and my love of the Florida I remember, and of its history and its old-timers.

Marvin Wilson, Terrene, Rosetta, & Latrell Pappy, all children of old Sampson families and descendants of many of the early settlers, Sampson, abt. 1946

Sampson

What ever happened to the community called Sampson in northwest St. Johns County? The boundaries were never definitely defined, but the historic community was roughly within the boundaries of US 1 on the east; Racetrack Road on the north; State Road 13 on the west; and County Road 16-A on the south.

Harriet Beecher Stowe sketched a crude map during her time in Mandarin (1867-1884) of the road between Mandarin and St. Augustine. Her map shows Sampson Road as well as Sampson and Diego (Palm Valley) Road, which are currently State Roads 210 West and East respectively.

Sampson is an old community by American standards. Descendants of earlier settlers of Sampson still live in the community, although it is becoming nearly unrecognizable to these rural families.

Sampson got its name from land reserved for James Samson prior to February 12, 1783, when Joseph Peavett received a British land grant of 500 acres on "Julianton and Durbin Creek near land laid out for James Samson" (Land Grant Records of Joseph Peavett from the Florida Memory Collection). It is not certain that Samson ever even came to Florida. Although the land was laid out for him, he was never the recipient of a land grant either confirmed or non-confirmed. Nevertheless, Sampson is a corruption of his name, and it is from the land reserved for James Samson that the area got its name.

Peavett's land grant is just a few hundred feet north of land my parents bought in 1945, and is still shown on maps today.

According to an article by Susan Parker in the *St. Augustine Record* of Sunday, January 26, 2003, Governor Patrick Tonyn of British East Florida, who allowed the Minorcans to leave Turnbull's plantation in

New Smyrna to find refuge in St. Augustine, had property adjoining that of James Samson. Tonyn had 1,000 acres on Twelve Mile Swamp south of Joseph Peavett's 500 acres. Parker wrote, "Peavett received full title to his acreage next to Sampson's property. Gov. Tonyn tried to acquire the title to his land near Sampson's property, but was unsuccessful. James Sampson apparently left Florida and made no formal attempt to claim title . . . ."

Parker found it ironic that the better-known Tonyn and Peavett (husband of Eugenia Price's title heroine Maria) were ignored while Samson left his name on the community.

From the description of the location of Tonyn's property, the 40 acres my parents bought in 1945, south of the Peavett grant, was once part of Governor Tonyn's 1,000 acre plantation. I now live on part of that property, as does my sister and several of our children and grandchildren.

One of the earliest residents of Sampson was Francis Pass. According to record MC31-62, on file at the St. Augustine Historical Society Library, Francis P. Ferriera was the administrator of the estate of Francis Pass. He stated Pass's residence was "at Samson, about 20 miles northwest of St. Augustine during 1812. He cultivated the land and raised cattle. Inventory of his losses (during the Patriot Wars) amounted to $9,085.00. Witnesses for this claim were Martin Canova and Joseph Papy. They described the way the Patriots and the United States troops took over the land and stole, butchered and burned the crops and the cattle." [Jose Papy was my great-great-grandfather.]

During the so-called Patriot Wars, America ran illegal campaigns against the Spanish citizens in the colonies of East and West Florida. President James Madison denied authorizing the war when it failed. American "patriots" from Georgia joined by some Spanish citizens of the Floridas attempted to seize the Floridas from Spain. During the Patriot War, on September 12, 1812, the Battle of Twelve Mile Swamp occurred. Twelve Mile Swamp is partially in Sampson. Letters from some of the invaders written to Americans were captured by the Spanish who won this skirmish and were sent to the Spanish Archives in Spain. (*Florida Historical Quarterly*, "Letters of the

Invaders of East Florida, 1812", Rembert W. Patrick, Vol. 28/1, pp. 53-65, July, 1949)

The St. Augustine News Extracts posted on Rootsweb.com for December 15, 1866, stated: Sampson Precinct No. 3, [polling place was] at the house of Alexander Powers. The postal inspectors were Robert Mickler, Alexander Powers, and Paul Sabate.

Alexander Powers and family were listed on the 1870 Census outside St. Augustine in Sampson. He was born in Appling County, Georgia, and was first listed on the St. Johns County census in 1860. He married Margaret Missouri Foster before 1870. Alexander and his first wife Mary Howard were the great-grandparents of my husband Yulee Mickler. Their daughter Susan married the first Yulee Mickler.

It is impossible to separate the Sampson residents from those of the other communities outside of St. Augustine included in District 22, St. Johns County, in the 1860 Census.

Sampson as listed on the 1870 Census may have had the largest population ever until recent years when developments have sprung up faster than weeds. The census (which may include some residents from some surrounding communities) lists Benjamin J. Self, 22 year old farmer born in Georgia; Antonio Mier, 23 year old Farmer born in Florida with his wife Mary and son Hutto; Benjamin Powers, 28 year old Farmer from Georgia with his wife Mary and daughter Florida; Alexander Powers, 58 year old farmer from Georgia with wife Missouri and children Harriet, Nancy, Alexander, Allen, & Susan; John P. Masters, 49 year old farmer born in Florida with wife Civility and children John, Civility, Catherine, Lizzie, Louisa, Margrette, and James plus three farm laborers: Amos Overstreet of Florida, Alick Martin, a black, born in Florida, and Bartolo Masters of Florida; Peter C. Masters, 35, mason of Florida; Bartora [should be Bonaventura] Masters, farmer, 26, of Florida, Eliza his wife, and children William, John, Mary, and Ella; Peter Falanny [Falana], 56, farm laborer born in Florida, wife Sarah, and children Emanuel, Peter, Mary, Caroline, & John; William Dukes, 45, farm laborer from South Carolina, his wife and children Charles and William; James and John Pope, farm laborers born in Florida; Hester Powers, 18, of Georgia; Davies Hogarth, 56 year old farmer from South Carolina, his wife Ann, son Charles, and a 25 year old laborer; Thomas

Simons, 80 year old black farmer born in Florida with Sepis Simons, black male, and Mary Simons, black female; Chas. H. Petterson, 56, farmer from Vermont with wife Elizabeth and children Eugenia and Willard; John Ashton, 17 year old farm laborer from Georgia; Caeser Weeks, 29 year old laborer born in Florida; Stephen Ferris, 35, lumbering, born in Florida with wife and children James, Julia, and Mary; Laurence Proctor, 25 year old black farm laborer; Ignacio Ortagus, 44, farmer born in Florida with wife Mary A. and children Mary, Antonio, Ignacio, William, Matilda, Aranie, Josephine, Tavista, and George; Paul Sabate, 45 year old farmer, born in Florida, wife Agatha, and children Francis, Mary, Susan, Christina, Gertrude, and William Gilby; Benjamin Moody, 39 year old farmer from Georgia with wife Louisa and children Isadora, Thomas, Alexander, Mary, Fanny, Benjamin, Joseph, Randel, and Jessie; Robert Mickler, 45 year old farmer from Georgia with wife Ruth and children Louis and Robert; Venancio Mier, 49 year old farmer from Georgia with wife Anita and children Tellana, Edward, Louis, Venancio, Rosa, John, & George; William A. Mickler, farmer from South Carolina with wife Manuela and his brother John, his wife Margarette and their children Mary, John, Camilla, and Anna; James Mickler, 43 year old farmer born in Florida and sons Robert and Weedman; John Smith, 16 year old farm worker from South Carolina; Isakiah Brown, 31 year old farmer from Georgia with wife Margaret and children Seaner (?), Nancy, and Fausa(?) and William J. Flino, age 10; William Railey, 35 year old farm laborer from Georgia, his wife Airena and children Martha, Morgan, & George; William Dickerson, 47 year old farmer from South Carolina, wife Elizabeth, and children Samantha, William, Martha, Ellen, John, Sarah, Henry, and Melinie; Berry Brown, 39 year old farmer from Georgia, his wife Ellenda and children Martha, Jane, Thomas, James, and Sake; Spicer Braddock, 40 year old farmer born in Florida, his wife Jane, and children Christopher, Foster, David, Oscar, Ruth, Hattie, and Hutto; Manuela Dove, 54 year old widow, a farmer born in Florida with her children Yulee, Robert, and Kate Mickler; Nancy Pope, 50 year old farmer born in Florida and her children Anna and George; Sary Galloway, a black farmer from South Carolina; Thomas Roberts, 30 year old farmer from England; Maria Black, 60 year old female farmer born in Florida with her family John, Frank, James, Geo. W., and Tonita; David Grey, black farmer born in Florida with Bobby, George, and Julia Black; Phillip Wanton, 55 year old farmer born in Florida; James Caviras (?), 30, farmer born in South Carolina, wife Nancy, and children Nancy, Sarah, & James; James Osteen, 30 year old farmer born in Florida, wife Margaret and children James and Susan; James Bridier, 60 year old blacksmith from New York, and Mary, George, and Sarah; Aunsly Hall, 40 year old farmer from Georgia, wife Mary, and children James, Ainsley, John, and Mary; Simon Beardon, 30 year old farmer from Georgia, wife Margaret and son James; Bernard Weedman, 28 year old farmer from Georgia, wife Susan, children Bernard and, Phillip; John Sirey, 40 year old farmer born in Florida, Jane and Margaret; John Robers, 50 year old male from Georgia with wife Amelia and children Mollie, John, James, Robert, Flora, Phillip, Francis and George. Following the Civil War the Sampson area had grown to 246 residents by 1870.

Sampson Cemetery was founded about 1875 by Jane Harvey Houston Braddock. She donated part of the property on which she lived for a cemetery, according to her great-grandson, Hugo (Bubba) Schill. The cemetery is now surrounded by St. Johns Golf and Country Club.

Jane Harvey Houston was born May 1, 1831, in Big Talbot Island, Duval County, Florida. She and her family lived in Yulee and Diego (now Palm Valley), Florida before moving to Sampson. Jane married Spicer Christopher Braddock February 13, 1851, in Duval County, Florida. Spicer Christopher Braddock was born December 25, 1829, in Evergreen, Nassau County, Florida. He died April 12, 1874, in Pottsburg Creek, Duval County, Florida. He was listed on the 1860 Slave Schedule in the 22nd District which was outside of St. Augustine in St. Johns County. This included Diego and Sampson, so it isn't sure in which community was their home at the time.

It is believed that the first burial (or burials) in the cemetery was an infant/infants of Jane and Spicer, that the grave/graves are unmarked, and that burial/burials occurred before the land was donated for a cemetery.

Descendants of Jane and Spicer Braddock still live in Sampson.

Children of John Masters intermarried with other Sampson families, and they, too, still have descendants in Sampson.

Ignatio Ortagus' large family also intermarried with other Sampson families, and he still has descendants living here today.

William A. Mickler was my great-grandfather on my mother's side. He and his brother John were famous scouts in Wade Hampton's South Carolina Brigade during the War Between the States and their exploits are immortalized in *Arab* by E. Prileau Henderson. (See "Confederate Scout . . .".)

Manuela Dove was first married to Jacob Mickler. They were the great-grandparents of my husband Yulee Mickler who was named for their son, his grandfather, the first Yulee Mickler. Jacob died in 1857 and following the War Between the States she married a Union officer, Captain Dove. Her family wouldn't accept him, and he returned north. Five of Manuella's sons fought for the Confederacy, and three died during the war. She also had at least one son-in-law in Confederate service.

The family of Maria Black lived at Black's Creek on 210 just west of Cimmarone.

In 1880, the following families lived in or adjacent to Sampson in St. Johns County Voting Precinct 3: Samuel Stratton; David Stratton; Paul Johnson; C.W. Grosenbacker; Henry W. Wilson, Antonio Ortagus; Ignatio Ortagus; C.F. Sallas; Andrew Huntley; Prudentio Ortagus; Isadore Ponce; Gertrude Melcher; O.F. Braddock; George A. Walker; William D. Braddock; Jane Braddock, C.S. Braddock; Ignatius Ortagus, Jr.; Jane Cubbedge; John Adams; Albert Cubbedge; Matilda McQuaig; John McQuaig; and Gordon McQuaig.

William Braddock was born in Sampson in 1851. His parents Oscar and Ann Bessant Braddock had come to Sampson from Nassau County, Florida. He married Matilda Ortagus. They were the parents of eleven children, at least three of whom were born in Sampson. Their son Leavy Francis Braddock is the grandfather of Verna Campbell who has a wonderful website with much genealogical information about old families of the area. Florida Braddock, daughter of William, married Charles Albury. Their grandchildren still live in Sampson on C. E. Wilson Road.

Samuel Stratton was a native of New York. He moved to Duval County, where he joined the Confederate Army in May 1861 and deserted a year later. Samuel married second a South Carolina girl, Rosa Cubbedge. They were the parents of at least five children. Their son Charles Dominion Stratton married the daughter of Isadore Ponce, Maria Ellen. Juanita Stratton Wilson is a descendant still living in Sampson.

David Stratton was Samuel's brother. He was also a native of New York. He married a Georgia girl who may have been a relative of his sister-in-law. Her name was Mary Cubbedge. David also joined the Confederate Army and served from October 1861 to July 1862, when he was discharged. They were the parents of at least four children.

Isador Bartalo Ponce was born in St. Augustine in 1846. He married his first cousin, Marcella Florida Ponce. He joined Capt. Phillip's Company B, "St. Augustine Blues", 3rd. Infantry, CSA at the age of 15 on August 17, 1862.

Jane Braddock, widow of Spicer, had four children from ages six to 17 with her: Ozilla, Hutto; Ruth; and Oscar Braddock. She was living on property adjacent to the cemetery.

Ozilla Braddock was the third wife of my great-grandfather Francisco Fertino Ponce. Francisco was twice widowed, first by the death of Mary Jane Pacetti Ponce, mother of my grandmother Rosalea Ponce Pappy, and second by the death of her sister Eugenia Pacetti Ponce, both who died young. Francisco and Eugenia were the great-grandparents of Juanita Stratton Wilson, a current resident of Sampson.

C. F. Sallas was actually Fabian Sebastian Charles Sallas and was apparently the builder of the house bought by my parents Terrell and Josephine Mickler Pappy in 1945. Fabian and Mary Sallas were living in Sampson by 1880, and were listed on the 1885 Florida Census as Phebian and Mary Salas. Fabian Sallas was born in Mayport, Duval County or St. Augustine, St. Johns County, January 20, 1844, and baptized in the Cathedral in St. Augustine. He was living in Duval County in 1860. He was a farmer. He married Maria de Merced Ortagus, daughter of Ignatio and Mary de la Merced Masters Ortagus in 1871 in the Cathedral, St. Augustine. Their children were listed on censuses as Joseph, Charles, Thadeus, Solomon, Emeline, and Josephine. In 1885 they were listed in Sampson between Isador Ponce and Antonio Ortagus, brother of Mary Ortagus Sallas and son of Ignatio Ortagus, on the census.

One afternoon about 1950 when my sister Terrene and I were playing in the front yard, two ladies who to my remembrance as an 11 or 12 year old were elderly, drove up in front of our home. They told us they were so happy to see that the old house was still standing and that children lived in it. They said that their father had built the house about 75 years previous. I thought they said their father's last name was Silas. No record could be found of any Silas living in the area, but when I saw the name Sallas listed in Sampson census records, I immediately realized this was the name of the man who built our house. He had two daughters according to the census of 1885: Emeline and Josephine Sallas. These were probably the ladies who had come to see their childhood home. (See "Daddy's Bargain".)

My parents purchased the old home and 40 acres from Eli and Gladys Herndon on October 5, 1945, for $300. The Herndons bought the place from Mamie Tart, widow of Edmund, February 2, 1942, for $10.00. Mamie Tart was issued a tax deed on June 5, 1939, for $30.66. She and Edmund Tart bought the place from S. A. and Ada Stratton for $1,100.00 on November 20, 1929. Edmund was from Canada and Mamie was from Pennsylvania.

By 1885, more families were living in or adjacent to the farming community of Sampson. There was the family of Oscar Braddock; William Braddock; Ignatio Ortagus Sr. and Jr.; Antonio Ortagus; Isadore Ponce; Phibean Salas (Fabian Sallas misspelled), all farmers. William J. Wilson had moved his family to Sampson from Nassau County, Florida. He was a logger. Also here were the families of Prudencio Ortagus, Jane Braddock; William Ortagus; Henry Wilson; Daniel Polk; Thomas Caldwell; Harrison Brooker; John Masters; Robert Mickler; Mary Powers; Thomas Foster; and Jacob Leppo.

Thomas Jefferson Foster was born in Georgia in 1856. He married Frances Civility Masters, the daughter of John P. and Civility Ashton

Masters. He was a county commissioner around the turn of the century representing the Sampson area.

William Braddock's daughter Georgia (Dautie) Braddock, born in Sampson in 1880, married Clinton Everett (Bussy) Wilson (born in 1875 in Nassau County, Florida), son of William J. Wilson. James Palmer Wilson, known as Palmer, another son of William J. Wilson, married another Sampson native, Laura Elizabeth Ortagus, daughter of Ignatio S. (Nacie) Ortagus and Emma Cubbedge. Some descendants of these families still live in Sampson today.

William J. Wilson was the son of James Wilson who was born in 1802 in Dunfermline, Fife, Scotland. He was living in Nassau County, Florida, by 1838, when he married Ann Ozilla Braddock.

Joseph B. Papy

Sometime between 1885 and 1892, Joseph B. and Louisa Henry Papy moved to Sampson. Joseph was born in St. Augustine February 3, 1830, and met Louisa while serving in the Confederate Army in Columbus, Muskogee County, Georgia. Joseph first moved his family to Florida in 1869, shortly after the birth of Marcus, born in Georgia March 5, 1869, and baptized in the Cathedral, St. Augustine, on June 21, 1869. In 1870, they were listed on the 1870 census, and apparently lived in the Mill Creek and Bakersville area of St. Johns County. Their son Robert was born in St. Johns County on April 29, 1870. They moved to Macon, Georgia, before May, 1873, where their son Francis was born. Their son Marcus married Rosalea L. Ponce on November 17, 1892. Their marriage

is recorded in St. Joseph's Catholic Church, Loretto, but they may well have married in the Sampson Church, a satellite of St. Joseph's.

Marcus D. Pappy

Marcus too, was living in Sampson by 1892, when his youngest sister Estella died of yellow fever and was buried in Sampson Cemetery. Joseph B. and Louisa Henry Papy were my paternal great-grandparents, and Marcus and Rosalea were my grandparents.

Clinton "Bussy" Wilson

In 1900, Sampson was listed as part of Precinct No. 17 on the census. The family heads living in or very near Sampson were Isador Ponce; Charles D. Stratton; Gregory Carrera; James Braddock, Aden Turner, Marion Wilson (widow of William); William D. Braddock; Rollin McNeil; John Houston; Edson Turner; Nathan Nabb; (also listed were some black families from Elwood at Leo McGuire Road and Road 16 which was not a part of Sampson); Christopher Braddock; Samuel Stratton; Ignatio Ortagus; Marcus Papy, Joseph Papy; Francis Papy; Joseph L. Papy; William Ortagus; John Norris; John McQuaig; Albert Adams; George W. Smith; George B. Adams; Matilda McQuaig; Frank Garnto; Willie McQuaig; John Pope; J. McQuaig; Mr. Cubbedge; Thomas James; Henry Wilson; B. Wilson; Patience Johnson; Thomas Russell; and Peter Falana.

Charles D. Stratton, the son of Samuel H. Stratton and Rosa Cubbedge, was born in Florida in 1874. He married a daughter of Isador Ponce, Maria Ellen, probably in the Sampson Church in 1893. Their marriage is recorded in St. Joseph's Catholic Church, Loretta, which had a circuit riding priest who took care of the Sampson mission. They were the parents of nine children. They lived on what is now C. E. Wilson Road immediately south of the church.

Rollin McNeil was born in Georgia about 1866. He married Adella "Bell" Ponce, another daughter of Isador Ponce, probably in the Sampson Church in 1892 (this marriage also recorded in St. Joseph's).

Gregory Carrera was a blacksmith, and he also did other kinds of work in metal. He lived in the old two-story house on C. E. Wilson Road now occupied by the family of Harold Lowe and previously by Daniel and Frances Braddock Smith. Carrera may have built the house. He was born in Picolata, Florida, in 1868, and married Christiana Braddock, daughter of Oscar Braddock, about 1888 in Clay County, Florida.

Samuel Alexander Stratton was the brother of Charles D. Stratton. He married first Lillian Braddock, daughter of Oscar Braddock. In 1900, the census reported Lillian was the mother of three children, two still living. Lily died in 1901, and Samuel married Ada Alice (last name unknown) about 1902. They had seven children. They lived in the house my parents bought in 1945. The name of their son Miles Stratton was carved into the walls of the old barn in several places.

At one time Sampson had a Church that was a mission of St. Joseph's Catholic Church in Loretto (now considered part of the larger community of Mandarin in Duval County). The Sampson church or chapel was in existence in 1907, when Father Bresnahan spoke of that mission in his book *Seeing Florida with a Priest*. He said the church no longer existed at the time that he wrote his book in 1937. The church once stood on what is today known as C. E. Wilson Road on the north side of County Road 210. It runs between E. W. Pappy Road and I 95. The church was between property homesteaded by my great-grandparents Joseph (Jose) B. and Louisa Henry Papy and property owned by Charles Dominion Stratton.

Father Bresnahan spoke of Marcus Pappy and Tony Octagus (sic, should be Ortagus) of Sampson in 1907 in his book. E. W. Pappy Road off 210 east of I 95 leads to the place where the Marcus Pappy family lived. It was inherited by their son Euzeal Worley Pappy for whom the road was named. The house that I remember that was home to my Pappy grandparents, built in 1906, burned down in the 1960s or '70s. One of their grand-daughters still lives on the property as well as some of their great-grandchildren.

The earliest marked graves in Sampson Cemetery are those of Janie Mier, born in 1873, died in 1889; Manuala Mier, born 1875, died 1889; Jane Houston Braddock (founder of the cemetery), born 1831, died 1892; and Estella Papy born 1883, died 1892. It is generally believed that at least one of the unmarked graves is older and that of a young child of Jane H. Braddock.

Bubba Schill and Josephine Mickler Pappy, cousins, each told me a story concerning the cemetery and their grandmother. Before the turn of the century, their grandparents William and Josephine Reyes Mickler lived in Sampson. There was an epidemic of some sort, and there were deaths in Diego (possibly the Mier children who died on the same day in 1889, in Diego). Sampson & Diego (Palm Valley) were closely associated, with families living in each community having relatives in the other community. In order to protect others from the disease, burials must be immediate, so the caskets were loaded onto a wagon and pulled by horses to Sampson for burial at night. There was no time to get the priest from Loretto. Instead, someone went ahead to ask Josephine to eulogize those who had died. Josephine was said to be a devout Catholic, the religion of most of those who lived in the area, as well as very intelligent, and a good speaker. She cut through the woods between her house and Sampson Cemetery to meet the midnight funeral party, and there officiated over the burials. [Josephine Pappy was my mother, and William and Josephine Reyes Mickler were my maternal great-grandparents.] It is believed William and Josephine lived on the south side of 210 and very near to the I-95 right of way.

Sampson Cemetery is a private cemetery, and only those whose ancestors are interred there are eligible for burial in it. It used to be reached by going from 210 down Leo Maguire Road until the road was cut in half for two housing developments that did not want through traffic for their communities. Now one has to turn on the newer Leo Maguire Parkway west of Leo Maguire Road and twist and turn through that community to get to the cemetery which is surrounded by a golf course. Four cemetery cleanings are held each year, and at the fourth cleaning of the year those in attendance have their annual meeting to discuss old business, introduce new, and to elect a board to take care of cemetery business for the next year.

Every year since 1986 until his death Msgr. Harold Jordan came from St. Augustine to the cemetery in November to say a Catholic Mass for the souls of those buried there. Since his death various priests have continued the annual Mass.

Sampson also had a school in the beginning of the century. It was near the corner of 210 and Russell Sampson Road. The building, donated by William James Wilson (1845-1900) to St. Johns County, still stands, and was the home of Earl and Eva Foster Wilson until a few years prior to Eva's death in 2002. Descendants of this family own the building, and it is currently occupied by the grandson of Earl and Eva Wilson. My father (Terrell J. Pappy) and his siblings attended school there. Daddy said he had to quit school after the fifth grade to work in the fields on his father's farm. Daddy also related that he walked the mile to school and that he and his siblings carried biscuits with mustard and plain biscuits they could dip into the cane syrup which they had buried in a jar in the school yard. This was their lunch.

An excerpt from an article in the St. Augustine Record, Tuesday, July 29, 1997, by Tiffany Merlo says this:

> . . . for those longtime residents who call the community home, Sampson means much more. Just ask 86-year-old Eva Wilson.
>
> If you continue on County Road 210 West and under I-95, you will see her small white house on the right side of the road.
>
> Her home was once a place filled with young, fertile minds waiting to be taught.
>
> It was a one-room school house for the neighborhood Sampson children many years ago.
>
> As Wilson's son, R.J. Wilson, tells it, his great-grandfather gave the land where his mother's house sits to St. Johns County Many years ago.

And that's when the school was built.

An old Sampson Public School end-of-the-term program from about 1908/09 lists the teacher as Grace Berry and the St. Johns County Superintendent as W.S.M. Pinkham. The children were born between about 1893 and 1902, suggesting the school was a first to eighth-grade school. The girls were Mary Ann Acosta; Mary Ellen Carrera (written in by hand); May Bell Wilson; Birty, Ethel, Florida, Frances, and Minnie Braddock; Florence Ortagus; Lorena Ogilvie; Laura and Ocia Pappy; Jennie and Ethel McNeil; Ila and Vada Wilds; Vonnie and Mildred Stratton. Boys were Emery, Zerney, Clarence, and Marcus Pappy; Arthur Carrera; Spencer and Craig Wingate; Clyde and Ashby Ogilvie; Louis and Vivian Acosta; George, Drew, and Marcus Ortagus; Christopher and Alcy Braddock; John McNeil; Theodore Wilds; Andrew, Rufus, Shelley, and Isadoria Stratton.

When the building was no longer used as a school, James Palmer Wilson (1881-1961) bought the land back, and he gave the place to his son Earl and his bride Eva Foster as a wedding gift. They were married in December 1831.

This is thought to be Peter "Posey" Foster and his bride Mary Florence "Mamie" Braddock by some of his grandchildren. The picture was found behind a mirror in the bedroom of their daughter Eva Foster Wilson. The original was once tinted and in a frame with an oval opening. He has a striking resemblance to some of Posey's grandsons. Photo courtesy of R. J. Wilson.

Earl James Wilson was the son of James Palmer Wilson and Laura Elizabeth Ortagus. Eva Louise Foster was the daughter of Peter Posey Foster (son of Thomas Jefferson Foster and Frances C. Masters) and Mary Florence Braddock (daughter of James Aldridge Braddock and Alice Ponce). Eva was born near Trout Creek, on the outskirts of Sampson. James Palmer and Laura Ortagus Wilson lived across 210 from the old school building occupied by their son Earl and his wife Eva.

The Foster family lived at Foster Hammocks. Foster Hammocks was on Trout Creek and Foster Creek, a branch of Trout Creek. You can no longer get to the area, because it is fenced off. It was on the west side of Leo Maguire Parkway (previously a part of Leo Maguire Rd.)

just north off the end of the paved road where there is a gate closing the road off. On the east side of the road was the Little Hammock. An old road crossed what is now Leo Maguire Parkway before the end of the pavement and on the east side crossed Dick's Ford somewhere about between Sampson Cemetery and I 95. On the west side it went through the Foster Hammocks and crossed 210 east of Black's ford. White's Ford was inside the gate at the end of Leo Maguire Parkway

In 1910, the name Sampson was actually listed on the census, and the usual surnames appeared in the community plus Acosta, Wilds, Williams, and Allen. The post office address for Sampson at the time was Durbin.

An article in the *Florida Times Union* on December 15, 1991, about my Uncle Emery Pappy (1902-1993) stated "There was a time, before the advent of game laws, when Pappy killed deer not just to eat but to survive . . . he grew up a farm boy near what is now the intersection of I-95 and 210 on land homesteaded by his grandfather.

"Pappy was one of 10 children . . . 'The family farm was about 15 miles from St. Augustine, 20 from Jacksonville, and the only way to get to either was by walking three miles to the railroad station. There were seven of us boys and we had to bring home something to eat,' Pappy said."

Apparently there was a railroad station at or near the end of 210 at U.S. 1 prior to the 1940s. There was definitely a side-track at 210 and & U.S. 1 where loggers brought their loads and loaded them on the cars for shipment.

Uncle Emery, born in Sampson like most and maybe all of his siblings, was a world champion skeet hunter. He won numerous state, national, and world championships and was inducted into the National Skeet Shooting Hall of Fame in 1991. There was also an Emery Pappy 28-gauge tournament held in Jacksonville in his honor.

In 1920, Sampson was listed in the census with the community of Durbin which was on U.S. 1 north of 210 near the St. Johns Duval County line. Besides the usual surnames there were Burney; Hertel;

and Dwiggins. Also listed were residents of Dixie Highway which is not in Sampson.

Louis Paul Ortagus was a resident of Sampson in 1920. He was the son of Antonio and Mary Ann Geiger Ortagus. He married a Michigan native, Martha Westbrook, and they had three children: Mildred, Lovett, and Norbert "Jack" Ortagus. Louis was a St. Johns County Commissioner representing the Sampson area in the 1920s. He lived on the Racetrack Road.

By 1930, the population of Sampson was about 50 people, and the only surnames were Russell, Ortagus; Masters; Foster; Wilson; Wilds; Townsend; Johnson; Pappy; and one black, a servant surnamed Rollins.

The 1935 Census lists Sampson in District 2, Bayard address. Heads of households with a Bayard address were the families of Marcus D. Pappy, Joseph L. Pappy, Eugene De Ray; Jim Mosely; Clinton Everett Wilson; Bernard Foster; C. A Wilson; E. A. Wilson, A. C. Wilson; J. Palmer Wilson; Tillman Pacetti, Edwin Wiles, Brahlford Gray, Isadore Stratton; Chas. D. Stratton; Roy Robinson; Dillon Stratton; Seabron Stratton; J. J. Smith; Travis Haymans; Clyde Smith; W. B. Bigby; Louis Ortagus; Jack W. Westbrook; Geo. B. Adams; John Adams; George Ortagus; William S. Goethe; Clarence and Curtis Russell; Mrs. A. G. Russell; Dewey Hicks; Clifton Wiles; Bernard Masters; Edmund J. Tart; Henry Ortagus; Nacy Ortagus; John Miller; J. M. Townsend; and Lucinda Stalls, all white. Blacks listed in Bayard were the George Ikner; Dave Pope; Willie Walker; Elliot Jones; C. J. Jenkins; and A. J. Jackson families. These men were section laborers. Other blacks were employed cutting cross ties and were Tom Houston; Arthur Cummins; Mack Wilkerson; James Williams; and Eddie Phillips.

By 1935 and during the 1940s, 1950s, and later the post office serving Sampson was Bayard in Duval County, and the address was Star Route, Bayard, Florida. *The St. Augustine City Directory 1940* lists the residents of Sampson along with the residents of the village of Hilden. It describes Hilden as "A village on the F.E.C. Railway, 14 ½ miles north of St. Augustine, the county seat and banking point. Mail delivery from Bayard." The names listed are:

Hicks, Dewey (Margt) driver
Laird, Herbert
Ortagus, Geo. Farmer
Pappy, Euzele
Pappy, Jos.
Pappy, Marcus
Percetti[sic], Harry, farmer
Robinson, Jas. J., laborer
Robinson, Kathleen (wid. Jas. J.)
Robinson, Roy S. (Helen), general Merchandise
Smith, Cath., Mrs.
Stall, Robt., farmer
Stratton, Chas. D., farmer
Stratton, Isadore (Thelma) farmer
Stratton, Seabron (Erma L.) laborer]
Stratton, Shelly T., farmer
Tart, Edmond J. (Mamie), farmer
Wilson, Alex A., farmer
Wilson, Clinton E., farmer
Wilson, Earl, farmer]
Wilson, Espy, farmer
Wilson, Herbert, County Commissioner
Wilson, J. Palmer, farmer
Wilson, Oscar (should be Oozie), farmer

Omitted from the Directory was the Raymond Mickler family.

During the late 18th and early 19th centuries, trains had Railway Post Office (RPO's) cars behind the locomotive. Facilities for receiving, sorting, and dispatching mail in transit were located in these cars. Mail bags were picked up from and hung on mail poles adjacent to the tracks near post offices in rural areas without the train having to stop.

Currently County Road 210 is the dividing line for whether the mail comes from St. Augustine (south side of 210) or from the new St. Johns Post Office in Fruit Cove (for residents on the north side of 210). Thus, some of us have a St. Augustine address, and the rest may use Jacksonville or the new St. Johns address.

Herbert Wilson was elected County Commissioner in 1938 and served our district as such until 1956. He was twice chosen to serve as chairman of the board. The year before his election, on June 22, 1937, Herbert's right foot was severely crushed when a cable on a pile-driver broke while he was working on the construction of the Palm Valley Bridge. His leg was amputated to just below the knee. About 1951, he was accidentally shot by a teenager while turkey hunting and struck in several places by 7 ½ shotgun pellets, resulting in his being blinded in one eye. In spite of these tragic occurrences, he was one of the most upbeat and happy people I've ever known. He had nick-names for everyone, and was always teasing and pulling pranks. He never lost an election, and retired due to his health. He was married to Phelza Ortagus. Their only child was stillborn.

Herbert Wilson, ca. 1950

The 1945 Florida Census of Sampson, with Willie Mickler, my grandfather, as enumerator, lists the families of Nickles Martin, Jamie Hartman, Carlos Hess, Carl Holt, O. C. Cowart; Lawson Cowart; Lewis[sic] Ortagus; Jessie Taylor; J. Lamb; C. R. Stephens; Clarence Russell; Curtis Russell; Liza Wilson; Battie Adams, Charles Clairr(?); C. H. Russell; Ben Russell; Henry Ortagus; Raymond Mickler; Palmer Wilson; Henry Bray; Herbert Wilson, Frances Smith; Hubert Pacetti; Shelton (Shelley?) Stratton; Marcus Pappy; and Joseph Pappy. Also listed in Sampson were the residents along U.S. 1 from 210 East (Palm Valley Road) to Hilden. Most of the men were farmers; women were housewives. There were also some whose occupation was listed as war workers, some members of the Army and Navy, and a few in various other occupations.

The Cowarts and Adams lived on or near Racetrack Road. The Cowarts had a dairy.

Shelly Stratton's family lived off C. E. Wilson Road north of 210 where Jim Arnold now lives.

The Raymond and Maude Mickler household, besides seven of their own children, included seven foster-children, four under a year of age; two aged four; and an eleven year old. There was also a 26 year old unrelated woman in the home.

Today, of all the old names once found here, only those with the Wilson, Albury, and Mickler names remain in Sampson, although Terrene Pappy Bennett, Ethel (Tiny) Pappy Casey, and I, whose maiden names are Pappy, still live here, we now bear the surnames of our husbands. Mr. Roy Robinson's grandson, Jim Arnold also lives in Sampson. Descendants of the Braddocks, Ortaguses, Strattons, Powers, Masters and other families still live here, though, and many of the early residents intermarried. We are mostly clustered around C. E Wilson, E. W. Pappy, Russell Sampson, and Terrell Pappy Roads. Many descendants of the early families live in Palm Valley, St. Augustine, Orangedale, Switzerland, and Jacksonville, Florida. Nearly all the other many residents of Sampson arrived during and after the 1990s, and still they come, yet most don't know that they live in Sampson.

During my childhood, the adults of Sampson were referred to as either Aunt and Uncle or Mr. and Mrs. Many of my aunts and uncles were not related by blood, but were close family friends, such as Uncle Earl and Aunt Eva Wilson, and Uncle Herbert and Aunt Phelza Wilson.

210 was a dirt road with deep ruts until it was paved about 1952 or '53. Electricity came to Sampson about 1953. Until then, Sampson was a community with outdoor privies and wells. Earl Wilson's well was made of cypress curbing hollowed out, 30" square and stacked on top of each other for the walls. Water was pulled up by a bucket on a rope, and everyone drank from the same gourd dipper. Our well had plank walls, and occasionally we would pull a snake up in a bucked of water. Later we had a well with a pitcher pump on our back porch.

Cooking was done on wood stoves which were also used as heaters by some families. Others had wood pot-belly heaters or fire places. Fuel was lightwood.

We ironed our clothes with cast iron irons. Maybe that's where the iron got its name. The irons were heated on the stove and rested there to keep them hot. Laundry was boiled outside in large cast iron pots over an open fire. Some women made their own lye soap. Clothes were hung on clotheslines, fences, or bushes.

Fruit and vegetables were canned, dried, pickled, and preserved. Meats and fish were salted in crocks, canned, and cured, or smoked.

Ice was bought in 25 lb. blocks, wrapped in newspaper for insulation and brought home in a wash tub. Those who had ice boxes put the ice there to keep food cold. Earl Wilson would split a 25 lb. block with his father. Both families had ice boxes.

Laura (Mrs. Palmer) Wilson had the first refrigerator in the neighborhood. It was kerosene and used 5 gallons a day.

The first electricity in the community was a 32 volt light plant which was used for running water and a wringer washing machine. It belonged to the Earl Wilson family.

Houses were lit with kerosene lamps. Most families had at least one Aladdin lamp, which was also kerosene, but instead of a wick, it had a mantle which was much brighter. You haven't studied or read a book unless you have done it by the light of a kerosene lamp. That's probably why most of us wear glasses or contacts now.

Women made quilts and no one had store bought blankets. At our house in winter, so many heavy quilts were piled on our beds, turning over resulted in a fight over covers or in quilts falling on the floor. We had no fire place, no heater, and the stove was only lit by Mama about 4 A.M.

Sugar cane was made into cider and molasses.

A few residents had gas stoves and refrigerators during the last few years before electricity. Animal hides were tacked inside-out on the barn wall (fur to the wall) and salted to cure. We had rugs made of dried deer hides on the floor by our beds.

Marcus Pappy sitting on a load of sugarcane; His daughter Ocia is standing on the left. About 1914, Sampson.

Grandpa Pappy, known as Pa to his children and Papa to his grandchildren, had chickens and pigs, grapevines, and fruit trees, and farmed for a living. He grew sugarcane, pumpkins, peas, beans and sweet potatoes among other things. When I was a child, he had a mule named Carrie that pulled a cart around the farm to haul his produce and also to pull his plow. Carrie was a stubborn mule, and was named for carrots which it loved to eat. Papa would tie a carrot to a string on the end of a pole, and dangle it in front of Carrie to keep her moving.

R.J. Wilson remembers helping the men of Sampson in clearing the right-of-way from U.S. 1 to our homes for Florida Power and Light Company to bring electricity to Sampson. They cut the right of way on the north side of 210 with crosscut saws and axes. Earl Tanner knew someone in Miami and he and County Commissioner Herbert Wilson got with him, and they got the poles to Bayard.

R .J. also remembers the first fire tower in the area. It was built on Maguire land. The top was cut from a large pine, and a little house was built on top of it with steps up the pine tree. Telephone wires were strung from Elwood across the woods to the tower so fires could be reported to the fire department. George Ortagus manned the tower.

Sampson was a farming community. Everyone had their own chickens, citrus trees and grape arbors. Many had pear, persimmon, pecan and mulberry trees.

All the children had chores before and after school. Terrene and I had chickens and pigs to feed and water before and after school, as well as helping on washday, ironing our own clothes, and helping with canning and cooking.

R. J. & Juanita Wilson; Latrell & Yulee Mickler, 2000.

Yulee Mickler and R. J. Wilson helped Palmer Wilson plant sweet potatoes. This had to be done in a drizzling rain. They cut the vines off root potatoes and planted the slips for 75 cents a day. Palmer sold a piled up peck of potatoes for 50 cents to the turpentiners.

Wood had to be cut for the stove; animals fed and watered, barns cleaned out, and other chores done, and around the Wilson barn R. J. and Yulee helped.

R. J. and Yulee were to remain best friends throughout their lives. Now widowed, I still count the Wilsons among my most treasured friends.

The Wilsons had cattle. There were sawmills and turpentine operations. The pines grew naturally and were widely scattered. You could see through the woods for a long way, because the trees were not close together, and the cattlemen burned the underbrush every year. Dead pine trees were used for lightwood, and that was the only wood used for wood stoves and fire places. Holes were made in trees, and turpentine crews would scoop the turpentine from the holes. Later, terra cotta cups were attached to pine trees to collect the resin for turpentine making. Hercules Stump and Powder Company blasted stumps of dead trees from the ground to use in the making of gun powder.

Mr. Mathis had a two ton truck. He had crews that he would put out in sections to gather the pine resin. They would put the resin in barrels and take it to a turpentine wharf. There were two wharves in the woods.

Workers would weed around the pine trees to keep fire from getting to them. The resin was extremely flammable.

It was not until during the 1940s that timber companies began reforesting Sampson, and it seems every replanting resulted in trees being closer together. Prior to that trees grew where they came up naturally. Someone from Maguire's went to Palmer and Oozie Wilson and told them the woods could no longer be burned because they were going to reforest. Oozie said, "You just come out here tomorrow, 'cause I'm going to burn the woods then." And he did, probably for the last time. Reforestation was another large factor in changing the way cattle were raised and resulted in many small-business cattlemen giving up the business.

Sampson was also a community of hunters and fishermen. The vast forests and swamps were home to turkeys, deer, squirrels, quail, and black bears. There were also panthers, wild cats, raccoons, gopher tortoises, fox, ducks, and other native animals and birds. (See "Quail Hunting . . .".)

Deer, though, were scarce due to screwworms, but since their eradication, deer have made an amazing comeback. Dipping vats were scattered throughout the area and cattle were driven to the vats and dipped in a creosote solution to kill the screwworms, and although this was very helpful to the cattle industry, it had little effect on the deer population.

Screwworms were the larva form of a certain blowfly. The flies laid eggs in wounds of cows and other warm-blooded animals and some form of blowfly also did the same in the gopher tortoise. The hatching screwworms ate the flesh of the host animal, with as many as a thousand or more eating at the same wound. This infestation could kill the cow or other infected animal.

The worms grew to about 2/3 inch long, and then they fell off to become pupa from which adult flies emerged sometime between 8 and 30 days, depending on temperature. The flies would mate and then the female blowfly would search for a wounded animal in which to lay eggs.

Screwworms caused millions of dollars of damage until the late 1950s when sterile males were released that resulted in the eggs of the females not becoming fertilized, and this has resulted in the control of screwworms, although occasional outbreaks still happen.

Train engines had cow catchers to sweep free-roaming cattle and other objects off the railroad tracks in order to avoid a train wreck. These were metal frames located on the front of the locomotives.

Cattle-gaps were located on country roads in place of gates to prevent cattle from leaving the area in which they were fenced after fencing became mandatory. These were metal grates over ditches that cattle would not attempt to cross for fear of stepping in the gap between the metal cross rails.

Old time residents had claim to hogs that bore their marks in the form of differently shaped cuts in their ears, and these roamed freely in the swamps and flatlands. They are the ancestors of the feral (wild) hogs now living in the remaining unsettled areas of Sampson. They occasionally wreak havoc in expensive lawns of the area's subdivisions.

Many disputes arose over hogs. Sometimes they resulted in someone's house being burned down and in at least one case, a dispute ended in murder as a result of "bad blood" between families over hogs.

In the early 1930s, Palmer Wilson and another Sampson resident had an argument over a hog. A little later, Palmer and his son Earl went fishing at the beach. They returned to find Palmer's house burned down. Howard Stalls happened by and saw it burning.

At that time what is now Russell Sampson Road continued across 210 and curved by the old voting house, continuing to Palmer Wilson's home. From there it went across what is now I 95 to the home of Oozie Wilson. Past Oozie's it forked, and one fork went to Bussy Wilson's and the other through Twelve Mile Swamp to Hilden. After Palmer's house was burned, he built a new house at the corner of 210 and Leo Maguire Road across from the old school house.

T. J. FOSTER IS SHOT AND KILLED - BAD KILLING OCCURS AT TROUT CREEK. - **Shot was fired From Ambush - Two Braddock Brothers Are Placed Under Arrest. –**

Waylaid and shot down from ambush within a mile of his home at Trout Creek, T. Jefferson Foster, Jr., a member of one of the best known families in St. Johns county, was the victim on New Year's morning of one of the worst killings that has occurred in the county. Charged with the crime, John and Fred Braddock, first cousins of the murdered man, are now held pending arraignment before the committing magistrate.

Early Saturday morning young Foster went out on horseback and drove up some cattle belonging to the family. One ox was missing and he remarked to his mother that he would go and hunt it up. He rode away on horseback towards the swamp less than a mile distant and that was the last time he was seen alive by his people.

As he had not returned by 7 o'clock when the morning meal was ready, the family breakfasted without him. A shot was heard but none gave any thought to it. A little later, however,

Mrs. Foster, his mother, saw the horse returning riderless and fearing that some accident had happened she rushed over to Mr. Willie Masters, one of the neighbors, and he and some others followed the horse's trail back to the swamp. The young man's father was in St. Augustine at the time.

They found young Foster lying by the side of the trail, dead and with buckshot wounds in his neck and right shoulder. Death probably followed the wounds instantly. It is supposed that he was fired upon from behind a cabbage palm tree close by him. The shot was fired very close to the young man as he rode along on horseback and it appears that he caught the full load.

Justice of the Peace W. R. Patterson of the Third District convened a coroner's jury and the jury returned a verdict yesterday to the effect that Foster came to his death by gunshot wounds inflicted by parties to the members of the jury unknown. Those serving on the coroner's jury were Messrs. Thomas Reddy, George Pacetti, C. S. Braddock, Ozzie Braddock, Vinton Pacetti and Rollin McNeil.

Chief Deputy Sheriff Raymond Sabate and Deputy Sheriff Joe Apler went to the scene of the killing yesterday and arrested the two Braddock brothers. They will soon be arraigned before County Judge Cooper for a preliminary hearing.

There has been old trouble between the two families, it is stated, and recently there had been more over some hogs. It is alleged that one of the Braddocks made threats regarding young Foster and this is probably much of the evidence that it is thought may connect them with the case. It is one of the most cold-blooded murders ever committed in the county and the sheriff's office is working hard to sift the case to the very bottom.

Foster is the son of former County Commissioner Foster and is well known throughout the northern section of the county especially. The killing has aroused much excitement in the Trout Creek and Durbin section. (Newspaper article, St.

Augustine Evening Record, 3 Jan. 1910, from Crime & Punishment Folder, St. Augustine Historical Society Library.)

My mother Josephine Pappy, Eva Wilson, and some of the other neighborhood ladies worked the polls at the old voting booth. I remember getting off the school bus on voting days and walking to the polls. Other neighborhood children would be there, too, and there was lots of pasture in which we would play.

In 1952 when General Dwight D. Eisenhower and Adlai Stevenson were the Republican and Democratic nominees for president, I remember my parents having a conversation about the vote count. One person in Sampson voted for Eisenhower; they couldn't believe that anyone in Sampson would vote for a Republican. Back then there were children and grandchildren of Confederate veterans living in Sampson. Reconstruction could still be remembered by some. Many families lost not only relatives, but property and all they owned during the war and reconstruction. They had a bad taste in their mouths concerning the Republican party. Later they learned that a man the entire neighborhood loved very much was the lone Eisenhower voter: Mr. Roy Robinson, a native of West Virginia.

Twelve Mile Swamp was a favorite hunting ground free to all until it was leased as a hunting club from timber companies that owned it, and even then the locals hunted there as members. More recently, part of the swamp has been or is slated for development, and some of it was bought by the St. Johns River Water Management District and is a Wildlife Management Area which currently charges $525 per member; members are chosen on a first-come-first-served basis with a membership option for renewal for two additional years. Once the community residents could fish and swim in the borrow pits and branches/creeks of Twelve Mile Swamp, but the management area is now closed except for hunting seasons, and then only open to members.

The flat woods also offered great hunting opportunities and were eventually organized into the Flat Woods Hunting Club which existed until Sampson was discovered as a desirable place to build developments, the first of which was Cimmarone.

Old time residents didn't welcome the developments, but there were so few of us, and the developments meant big taxes to the state and county. We didn't have a chance against them. Now that Sampson is ruined as far as we old-timers are concerned, the newcomers are here in such numbers that their voices will be heard. But to those of us whose families have lived here for generations, it is too late for more houses and people to make much difference to us. The Sampson we knew is mostly history. Now the newcomers can group together to prevent us from continuing to live as we always have, or to do as we wish with our property, especially if we should decide to sell due to increases in property taxes or the desire to live in a more rural community as we are used to. They can protest the development of our property, because it is all that is left outside Twelve Mile Swamp Management Area (and land not already sold for development by timber growing operations) that is truly rural Sampson. Due to the numbers of new residents, they will probably be successful in their protests where we were not.

R.J. Wilson tells of driving the family's cracker cattle to the marsh with his father, grandfather, and Uncle Oozie, cow hunting, rounding up and driving the cattle back to Sampson in the spring. They always carried a single shot .22 rifle and were accompanied by dogs which would find unmarked hogs and fox squirrels which they would kill and bring home to eat.

The cattle were driven to the marsh late in the year to feed on the bull rushes and marsh grasses. They had a cow camp at Sweetwater, which was north of Pine Island Road in what is now Nocatee. The cows were driven from Sampson to the Nocatee area where they were left until about March to roam the area from the marsh near the Palm Valley Bridge on the east to almost the old brick road known as Old Dixie Highway on the west, and from Hilden on the north to Pine Island Road on the south. Then, every morning before daylight except school days, R.J. would leave Sampson on horseback to help with cow-hunting, returning home nightly after dark. He said their behinds would feel like chopped liver from riding all day.

They would stop at Mr. Roy Robinson's House Jack Built to buy bologna and sardines for lunch. During the day when they were thirsty, they removed turpentine cups from pine trees and drank water that had collected in them, and then refastened the cups to the trees.

The pine tar would be hardened in the bottom of the cup and couldn't mix with the water.

R. J. Wilson with some of their cracker cattle, courtesy of R. J.

The cows were rounded up and penned at Sweetwater to be marked and branded before returning to Sampson in March. They were marked with a cut in their ear that was registered at the courthouse as well as branded with a mark burned into their hides. They drove the cows home across U.S. 1 near the House Jack Built, through Twelve Mile Swamp and across Oozie Wilson's place and then to their home pasture.

Before the cattle were driven home, the Wilsons would burn all the woods where their cattle roamed in the summer. This allowed new grass to grow for the cattle to graze.

Around Cabbage Swamp, trees would rot and leave holes in the ground. Cows would step in the holes, couldn't get out, and would die there. They would also fall into the holes left when stumps were blown out of the ground. Cattle would sometimes eat moss and get their heads caught in the forks of trees and die. In the marsh there were hard trails the cows followed to eat the bull rushes, but sometimes they'd get off the trail, bog down in the mud, and die.

During the summer, some of the cows would roam to the St. Johns River to eat hyacinths, and they'd have to go there to round them up.

**J. Palmer &
Laura Ortagus Wilson;
photo courtesy of R. J. Wilson.**

At the end of summer, when the cattle were in their best shape, steers would be sold. Mr. Vic Chauvin had a slaughter house on U.S. 1 south of the English Pub on the left just south of Atwood's Ditch and would buy the steers. Later Wilson sold his cattle to Mr. Snyder. "Mr. Snyder and Pa would walk around the cow pen. Pa wanted $30 a head for his steers. 'I be damn, Palmie, times is hard. I can't pay but $25.' Mr. Snyder would say.

"They'd dicker for hours and finally Mr. Snyder would offer $27. After the deal was made, Pa would say, 'That's the most I ever made in one day in my whole life.'"

It was only after the population of Florida got to a point that too many accidents were caused by cows on the roads that it became necessary to have a law mandating the fencing of cattle. When the fence law was enacted, the Wilson's fenced from Maguire Road to Container's property to Wolfe's Ranch. Herbert Wilson sold all his cows that were over by Racetrack Road. Palmer, Earl, and R. J. Wilson, and C. W. Albury went over there through thick yellow flies and got the cows. They brought them back and put them in the fenced pasture. Lightening struck a tree, jumped to the fence, followed the barbed wire, and killed three of Herbert's cows that were feeding with their heads under the fence.

After Mr. Palmer got too old to ride horses, they put the horses in the cow pen and carried their saddles back and forth to the horses every day in a 1939 truck until some mean men who called themselves hunters killed a cow over by the cemetery, cut her hams off, and left her. That was the straw that broke the camel's back for cattle-raising as far as Earl Wilson was concerned, and he decided it was time to quit with the cows.

Marsh tackies (cracker horses) also roamed the marshes in times past. The Wilson's owned one of them at one time, too. Its stomach was accidentally cut open on a stump; Mr. Palmer put a blanket around its stomach to hold the insides in, brought it home and sewed it up himself. Both the cracker cattle and the free-roaming horses, descendants of Andalusian horses, were brought by the Spanish to Florida. The cracker horse was recently named Florida's state horse.

Russell Sampson Road was previously known as Mickler Road from the 1930s until about the 1980s when the county decided to rename it Russell Sampson Road, because there were already several Mickler Roads in the county. Prior to that it was called the Sampson Julinton Road on one census. The current name was chosen because the Russell family had lived at the Race Track Road end, and the southern end was the center of Sampson. It was not named for a person named Russell Sampson as some believe. It should be considered a combination of the surnames of James Samson and that of the Russell family. 210 West was historically known as Sampson Road.

An old survey map from 1849 shows the Russell Sampson Road existed even then, and it appeared to be a part of the Fatio Road which apparently connected Fatio's grant in Sampson with Hilden to the east (this may have been the same old road the Wilsons used to drive their cattle to and from their winter grazing). It continued from the Fazio grant to the northwest following approximately the same route as Russell Sampson did before rerouting at both ends.

Russell Sampson Road is currently being rerouted on the southern end which connects with 210, and the old part which will no longer connect with 210 will be a private drive renamed Eva Earl Road for Eva and Earl Wilson whose family trust owns the property. 210 was previously known as Sampson Road.

Earl & Eva Foster Wilson; photo courtesy of R. J. Wilson.

Black's Creek goes into Trout Creek. Water from the Russell Sampson Road/210 area previously ran off in two directions: to Trout Creek and into Sampson Branch and eventually to Julington Creek. Cassina Pond was in what is now St. Johns Forest. It drained through Horseshoe Circle off Russell Sampson and then back to Sampson Branch. It was filled in for St. Johns Forest, and is now covered by houses. The water can no longer drain off and stands on neighboring property.

I can remember when there were uncapped artesian wells in the woods. One well was about a mile and a half from Bowen Branch and another was not far away, south of the Racetrack Road and west of Russell Sampson, about a mile from Julington Creek Cemetery. There was also a dipping vat for cows in that area, and the family of Dewey and Margaret Ortagus Hicks lived near there before they moved to Hilden.

Old corduroys forded the more shallow branches. These were logs layed down crossway the road to keep the horses and wagons, carts, or carriages from sinking into the mud. One was at White's Ford which was on the Leo Maguire Road halfway to Elwood from 210. Another was at Willy's Crossing. An old road once extended from the dead end of Terrell Pappy Road into what is scheduled to become Russell Sampson Road PUD and crossed Sampson Branch at a place known to old-timers as Willy's Crossing by the old Falana place. The road continued across what is now I 95 and across the north end of what is now C. E. Wilson Road where Great-Grandpa Papy lived, passing immediately north of E. W. Pappy Road behind Grandpa Marcus Pappy's house. There was a corduroy behind Grandpa Pappy's. The old wagon road continued on to U.S. 1 near Durbin. The road connected the old homesteads with one another and with the railroad. It was most likely used for logging purposes, too. Many of the old roads began as logging trails.

There were also natural springs in different places in Sampson. There was a small spring in Sampson Branch just east of my parent's' property line, and other springs in various places in the woods.

The Conservation Corps also created a road in Sampson in the vicinity of White's Ford to the Cemetery and out into Cummer's property. They are also believed to have dug ditches to Sampson Branch, one of which crosses Wilson property and goes under Russell Sampson Road at the end of Terrell Pappy Road into the creek, and another that divides Wilson property from the homestead bought by my parents in 1945 and goes from Terrell Pappy Road east to the creek.

Greenbriar Road, immediately west of Sampson, was called Airport Road and Bombing Range Road. The navy had a bombing range on the south (Switzerland) end of the road near 13. The area was called Pinehurst. North of Airport Road near 210 a road went to the Harvey place. That property is now a rehabilitation center for alcoholics. West of and near the Harveys was the infamous Anhorn place.

The 1920 census lists Albert[sic] Anhorn and his daughter Minnie Kemp in Switzerland, Florida. J. F. Elbert Anhorn was born in the country of Switzerland, was an 83 year old widower, and Minnie, born in Indiana, was 41 and divorced. Minnie's two sisters, Gertrude, 49, and Fannie, 46, also born in Indiana, lived nearby. They were both listed as widows, and there were two male boarders in their home.

The Anhorns owned more than 300 acres of land near Fever Hammocks at one time, and ran Pinehurst Seminary. The seminary was said to have been a school for unruly boys. When Elbert Anhorn died in 1921, and his daughter Fannie died in 1925, their bodies were not buried but kept in sealed coffins, and it is said Minnie slept between the coffins. She also kept the body of their black caretaker, George Riley, deceased in 1923, in a wooden coffin over buckets of limestone in an outbuilding.

Gertrude and Minnie guarded their property and the bodies with guns for 20 years, and people who approached their home were greeted with a woman pointing a rifle at them.

In an October 30, 1983 article in *The Florida Times-Union Jacksonville Journal*, Judy Hood Falana said she remembered hearing the Anhorns kept a bull in a small pen while the other cattle roamed, because the bull had "raped" a heifer.

Former students told the Journal reporter that the boys "worked like slaves in the fields and groves and with the livestock and at night slept in the barns or anywhere else we could find." A former student, Al Humphries, said Miss Gertrude draped a whip around her neck, and that he had been whipped with it many times before he ran away. He said she could crack the whip faster than silent-movie star William S. Hart could draw his gun.

Theodore Flynn said Miss Gertude was known to love creatures and was unable to bury anything she loved.

Gertrude was found slumped over a wheelbarrow nearly starved to death, and Minnie was also in bad condition in late September 1941 by a neighbor. Minnie wouldn't let her in. Gertrude died in a nursing home about three weeks later.

Their sister, Mrs. Bacheller from Rhode Island, had the caretaker buried in an Orangedale Cemetery, but had a harder time "prying the dead from Miss Minnie, whose mind was so affected . . ." J. F. Elbert Anhorn and daughter Fannie Cornelia Anhorn were buried Nov. 29, 1941, by Craig Funeral Home in Evergreen Cemetery, St. Augustine, Florida.

During my childhood, the Anhorn place was said to be mysterious and haunted, and all kinds of weird things were said to have occurred there.

Recently R. J. & Juanita Wilson drove me as close as it is possible to get to the home of the eccentric Anhorn sisters' place. It is now owned by I. T. T. Rayonier and is fenced and covered with pines.

I can remember the delight we felt as children when a hurricane nearby meant the roads would be under water, and being able to splash and play in the tannin stained water that ran over the white sand roads.

Sampson Branch was the neighborhood swimming and fishing hole. I remember the water in Sampson Branch running under the old wooden bridge on 210 so swift and deep that it touched the bottom of the bridge. My husband told of him and his brother Charles jumping from the bridge into the fast current and riding it down the creek and around the curve.

I often heard panthers screaming like women in the night from my upstairs bedroom window. I read somewhere recently that these were the mating calls of the female panthers. I also remember seeing one of these stealthy creatures with his long curving tail cross the dirt road leading from our house when we were on our way to catch the school bus one morning about six o'clock.

In the late 1940s and early 1950s, we had a neighborhood gathering place on Daddy's property near the edge of Sampson Branch where many of our relatives, neighbors and friends gathered on Sundays. It consisted of a tin-roofed shed built with the help of the same people, with picnic tables. While the women fried fish or cooked gopher stew, the men played poker and the children played ball, or fished in the edge of the creek, or just roamed in the woods. During baseball season, Herbert Wilson would pull his car up close to the poker game and turn the radio on to hear the ball game. Dr. Herbert White from St. Augustine and other city folks loved to join us at the camp. There was always whisky for the adults, including moonshine; cold drinks for us kids (a rare treat) and for mixing with whisky for the adults; and snacks to enjoy while supper was cooked in cast iron pots over an open fire.

Before the camp, many Sundays this same group would gather in our yard for a gopher stew, oyster roast, or fish fry with a friendly game of poker.

I vaguely remember going to cock fights at the home of Clinton (Bussy) Wilson as a very young child. I don't know whether it was legal then or not. Since we lived ½ mile from our nearest neighbor, any time there was a gathering entire families were present, and we had other children to play with. It was all great fun to us children.

We attended Mill Creek School, a four classroom, eight-grade school. "Aunt" Phelza Ortagus Wilson drove the bus, and we had to walk ¼ mile to Mickler (now Russell Sampson) Road to catch the bus which arrived about 6 AM. The bus ride to Mill Creek took a circuitous route picking up children along the way, was only allowed to go 40 miles per hour, and arrived at school about 7 AM. The parochial school children could ride the county buses then, too, and all grades rode the same bus. Those going to parochial or high school changed buses at Mill Creek for another hour's bus ride to St. Augustine. High school was Ketterlinus on Orange St. in St. Augustine. It is now an elementary school. We got home from school about 4 PM. Both before and after school the chickens had to be watered and fed, and when we had hogs in the pen, they had to be slopped and watered.

Phelza Ortagus Wilson; Leatta Wilson Pappy; a sister of Georgia Braddock Wilson (Ethel or Frances); Georgia B. Wilson; Gertrude Wilson Pacetti; unknown in back; & Irene (wife of Everett Wilson), Sampson residents. Photo courtesy of Verna Mae Campbell.

Before Phelza Wilson drove the bus, Earl Wilson was the bus driver. An old bus schedule is among clippings and papers saved by his wife listing the names, approximate grades, times of pick-up and return of each child who rode the bus. He left home at 6:25 A.M., picked up Annie C. and Virginia Mickler 1 ½ miles away at 6:30, and returned them home at 4:30 P.M. This was his first and last stop of the day. Other students in order of pick-up were

Earl Wilson, school bus driver; photo courtesy of R. J. Wilson.

Elsworth Ortagus; Ronald Wilson, R. J. Wilson; Ernest and George Harvey, Joan Ortagus; Marjorie Ashe; Mary F. Apeler; John Roberts; John Black; Vista Lanier; D. C. and Jane Mosley; Donald Mulligan; Asa, Hedrick, Helen, Margaret, Merdice, and Millicent Fischer; Lavonda Pacetti, Edsel, Ellis, and Elsie Moody. School started at 8:00 A.M. at Mill Creek, and the high school students changed busses at Mill Creek to continue on to Ketterlinus High School in St. Augustine. The trip to Mill Creek was 21 miles and they arrived at Mill Creek at 7:35. The year is not stated, but it was approximately 1940.

Mama, too, drove a school bus for many years, starting about 1955. She loved all children, and they loved her. She drove a different route than Herbert and Phelza Wilson drove. She drove the route formerly driven by Margaret Ortagus Hicks, and she also took the kids from Mill Creek to Ketterlinus in St. Augustine.

**Josephine Pappy,
School bus driver.**

Mama went to work at Caspar's Alligator Farm on U.S. 1 north of St. Augustine when I was about 12. After that, Terrene and I had to start supper before Mama came home. Once she left a bushel of hard pears for us to prepare for canning. I cut my thumb to the bone, and Terrene and I could not stop the bleeding. We walked to the home of "Aunt" Eva and "Uncle" Earl Wilson, taking turns keeping compression on the cut to slow the bleeding. Aunt Eva grabbed a fistful of cobwebs from a tree and held my hand under the kerosene spigot. Then she put the cobwebs on the cut. The bleeding stopped. She convinced us to stay there until our parents got home. Mama was terrified to see the bloody trail and our footprints on the road, and followed them all the way to the Wilson's thinking all kinds of terrible thoughts about what might have happened to us.

Penicillin came into widespread use during World War II, but during my early childhood, it was practically unheard of in Sampson. Also, people, especially those in rural areas, didn't go to the doctor for what they considered minor ailments for which they had folk remedies.

The treatment for a red streak up the leg from stepping on a nail, a cut, or other infection was Epsom Salt. The infected area would be soaked in hot water with Epsom Salt dissolved in it or an Epsom Salt poultice – a heel of bread with Epsom Salt dampened and applied to the wound and held in place by a rag bandage left on overnight. By morning, the read streak would be gone.

Once I stepped on a broken glass cup from my cousin's tea set at my Grandfather Pappy's house in the early 1940s. I nearly cut my big toe off. Dr. White happened to be there, and he was very upset with me. He opened his doctor's kit and took out a bottle of expensive liquor and poured it on my foot to kill the germs, fussing the whole time about having to use his liquor that way. Then he bandaged my foot with sterile bandages from his kit.

Ground itch was a common ailment for us in summer, as we all went barefoot around our homes. The treatment was a purple pill that was dissolved in boiling water, and the feet were plunged into the water barely below the boiling point, it seemed.

Eugene Athlete "Oozie" Wilson, courtesy of R. J. Wilson.

Neighborhood kids would sometimes gather in the field of Earl and Eva Wilson for a baseball or football game during the summer when relatives from town provided enough kids for a game. Dried cow patties were bases and home plate for the base ball games, and sometimes they were ammunition to throw at each other.

When R. J. Wilson graduated from high school, the draft was still in effect. He didn't want to go into the army, so he signed up for the navy. When it came nearer to time for him to leave, his great-uncle Oozie Wilson said, "R. J., you don't have to go."

R. J. said, "Uncle Oozie, I *do* have to go. If I don't, Uncle Sam will come get me."

Uncle Oozie said, "Who's Sam? Damn Sam anyway. I'll take you back in the swamp and hide you in a stump and Sam won't ever find you."

R. J., knowing Uncle Oozie liked to go on a drinking spree now and then, said, "But Uncle Oozie, what's going to happen to me if you go off on a toot? You'll forget me and I'll starve to death."

Uncle Oozie said, "No, son, I won't forget you. I'll take care of you."

R. J. said, "Uncle Oozie, I know very well what you'll do. You love your cattle more than anything, but you forget them when you go off on a toot."

Another time, Oozie bought 10 or 15 head of pure-bred Angus cows from Freddie Francis. Sidney Mills came to fill out the registration papers. Sidney asked, "Oozie, how do you spell your name?"

Oozie answered, "E-U-G-E-N-E you damn fool. How do you think you spell it?" Sidney, like most folks, had never heard him called anything but Oozie.

If you had a cow and he got down, he usually died. To try to save the cow, old-timers would put croaker sacks under it and lift it up to stand, then lay him down, and prop him back up, etc. If the cow survived he would hate you, according to R. J. He would follow you around trying to get you. Oozie, Alec, and Bud Wilson had one such cow that they had saved. It got after Alec, and chased him around the kitchen a couple of times, and they threw a frying pan at it. It got Alec on one side of a tree with its horns on either side of the tree. Alec grabbed the horns, one arm on each side of the tree, and they went 'round and 'round the tree. Finally he hollered for Oozie to come help. Oozie said, "You caught him Alec, you ought to be able to let him go."

Eva Foster who married Earl Wilson went to school at Hardwood Landing. From Foster Hammocks she and her sister Madeline rode in a buggy pulled by a mule through the woods that bordered Trout Creek for about two miles to school. They'd unhook him from the buggy and tie him up at school. At the end of the day, they'd hook him back to the buggy and ride home.

A Mr. Miller lived on Miller Road which goes by the fire station. He was possibly John Miller, an Indiana widower who was living in Sampson in 1935. Miller's Bay is north of 210 and east of the CVS Pharmacy.

Elwood Maguire had a turpentine wharf on the north side of 210 near Cartwheel Bay, and the Joneses had a turpentine wharf off 210 on Road 11, later Camaro Road, and now Ashford Mills, next to Timberlin School. It was called Jones Turpentine Still, but pine tar was not distilled there. The resin was brought there in barrels and sent to a distillery in Jacksonville.

The settlement of Elwood at the other end of Leo Maguire Road was probably named for Elwood Maguire who employed the blacks who lived there in his turpentine business. Maguire was an ancestor of former St. Johns County Commissioners, twins Craig and Bruce Maguire.

My husband Yulee Mickler lived with his parents Raymond and Maude Newman Mickler, siblings, and many foster-siblings on what was then Mickler Road, now Russell Sampson. The house is now owned by the Wheelers and is next to Liberty Pines School. The house was said to have been previously occupied and built by an Ortagus. The Micklers moved there about 1937. Yulee was one of twelve children.

His mother cared for more than 500 foster-children for Catholic Charities from about 1920 until her death in 1967. The home in which they lived still stands on Russell Sampson Road near the new Liberty Pines Elementary School. (See "One Heroic Catholic Family").

The Wheeler home was once occupied by the Raymond Mickler Family. It is one of the oldest homes in Sampson.

Sometime during the 1930s, Revenue agents busted the largest moonshine still ever discovered in the state of Florida in Twelve Mile Swamp, Sampson. The owner of the still was never found; he was Hubert Pappy, brother of my father. In his later years, Uncle Hubert loved to talk about the years he was a bootlegger. He and my father and their brother Euzeal (pictured) were all involved in the business at the time the still was busted, but none were ever caught.

[The panoramic view on the following page is of Hubert Pappy's still, the largest ever discovered in Florida. Note the pigs on the left side of the picture used by the revenuers to sniff out moonshine stills. Pigs would often find stills and eat the soured mash, a byproduct of the whiskey which would make them drunk.]

Latrell Pappy Mickler

After World War I, in February 1919, their brother Clarence came home from service in the army, and went to work in a canning factory. Then came the post-war depression (1920-1922) coinciding with the beginning of prohibition in January 1920, which lasted until December 1933. Uncle Clarence went into the moonshine business about 1920, enlisting his teenage brothers Terrell and Hubert to work at his still near their home in Sampson. They learned the business at the ages of 16 and 14 respectively, and two years later when Hubert was 16, he visited the sheriff of a neighboring County where he was allowed to set up a still and buy the sheriff's protection. Subsequently he had stills at different times in Flagler, Volusia, and St. Johns Counties. At some point, Euzeal also began working for him.

Prohibition made the making of illegal whiskey a profitable business, and the post war depression followed by the great depression (1929-1940) resulted in men doing whatever they could to feed their families. Many men drank the illegal liquor to help them cope. During this time, the Pappy brothers were among those who made their living bootlegging corn liquor.

Buried treasure in Twelve Mile Swamp? That's what an old legend I first heard from my brother in law Charles Mickler says. Deep in the swamp there is a place where compasses are not reliable. The needle spins and a correct reading cannot be given. According to the legend, English soldiers fleeing the Spaniards buried their heavy chests of treasure in Twelve Mile Swamp. Was this possibly in 1702 when Colonel Daniel and Governor Moore of Georgia attacked St. Augustine by sea, but were forced to flee overland when four Spanish warships from Cuba appeared? The invaders had burned 118 homes and looted the city while the inhabitants were holed up in Castillo de San Marcos which the English were never able to penetrate. All I can say for sure is that my husband and sons have also hunted that place in Twelve Mile where compasses are of no help in determining direction.

About 1947, Miss Anna Heist, Home Demonstration Agent for St. Johns County, came to Mill Creek School to see Mrs. Thelma Pacetti (the best teacher St. Johns County ever had in my opinion, and possibly the best in the state) about starting a 4-H Club there. She asked Mrs. Thelma to be her assistant. Mrs. Thelma agreed on the condition that students in her class could join although the age limit was 10 and her students were eight and nine year olds. She could not leave the class unattended for meetings that were held at school, so by special permission we were allowed to join at age 8. The entire class became members. Some came from families who had cattle, and took raising cows for show as a project; others came from farms and took vegetable growing projects; some raised chickens which they entered in championship competition; others, myself included, took sewing. Later I also grew a few vegetables and engaged in a public speaking project for which I won a trip to the Florida State Fair in Tampa.

When I was 13 or 14, I entered a contest to sew articles from feed sacks. For this project I made clothing, a doll, and household items from white and printed feed sacks and an envelope purse from a croaker (burlap) sack. I was selected winner over St. Johns County and then over the five county district of St. Johns, Clay, Duval, Nassau, and Putnam Counties. I was, however, disqualified in the state competition, because Miss Heist, well up in age by then, had not filed all the necessary papers. The prize was an electric sewing machine, and since we had just gotten electricity, I so wanted it. Mama felt so bad for me, she bought a White-Westinghouse electric machine for us.

Most Sampson kids at the time were 4-H Club members. It was something we were well equipped for and was also a social club. We went to 4-H Camp at Cherry Lake in Madison County every summer for a week on a school bus, and the County Commission paid for our stay at camp. At camp we were assigned to cabins, about 10 girls per cabin.

Some years the camp was all girls with the boys going at a different time, and some years both girls and boys attended camp at the same time, but were separate on different sides of the camp area as far as cabins were concerned.

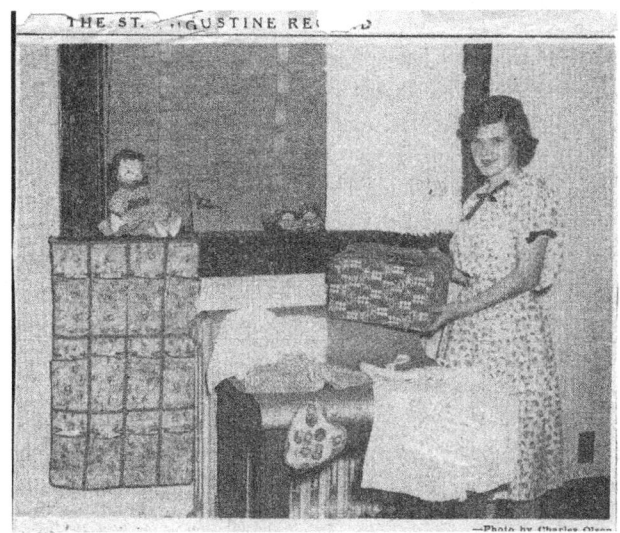

Photo from *The St. Augustine Record*. Beneath the photo states: A MILL CREEK 4-H CLUB GIRL WINS AREA COMPETITION, with recognition going to Latrelle(sic) Pappy of St. Johns County. Latrelle's exhibition of articles, made from cotton bags, has [been] selected as the best in an area competition in Jacksonville February 3. There were five counties in this area eligible to compete: Nassau, Duval, Clay, St. Johns, and Putnam.

The purpose of the 1952-53 "Sew With Cotton bags" project for 4-H Club girs was to encourage girls to make good use of what they have such as cotton bags. The girls who participated learned to select, prepare, and use cotton bags in the making of clothing accessories and household articles. Each entrant had to exhibit a minimum of eight articles and not more than twelve.

Latrelle Pappy is shown above modeling the dress she made of cotton feed sacks, and showing her winning exhibit. She has worked under the supervision of Miss Anna Heist, Home Demonstration agent, for four years, making many attractive and useful articles from sack materials.

This exhibit was selected to represent the area in the State Cotton Bag Exhibit to be held later this year.

We started the day at the flag pole where we saluted the flag and said the Lord's Prayer. We were taught crafts, took swimming lessons, helped prepare our food, cleared the tables, washed the dishes, cleaned our cabins, learned to square dance, and worked all week on a skit that each cabin's occupants performed the last night of camp.

Older members were selected yearly to represent the county at Florida State University for a week of what was called Short Course. I was selected to go at ages 14, 15, and 16 along with Beverly Simmons and Ann Mills and a couple of other girls. At Short Course, we signed up for hour-long short courses from a selection of interests and stayed in college dormitories. One year at Short Course we were taken on a tour of the governor's mansion, but the governor was absent that day. Another year we went to Wakulla Springs and took a glass-bottom boat tour of the springs where part of "The Creature from the Black Lagoon" was shot. These were all opportunities for learning, socializing, and expanding our horizons many of us would never have had if not for the 4-H Club.

The 4-H club also sponsored dances for members. It was a wonderful opportunity for country kids and still is, and is now also popular for city kids.

Tragedy struck in Sampson on the evening of June 23, 1955. Emma Jane Papy, wife of Joseph L. Papy, my grandfather's brother, was burned to death when their home was burned to the ground. Uncle Joe, then 79 years old, said he went into the bedroom to fill and light his pipe. Then he joined his wife in the living room. Shortly after, they saw smoke and found the bedroom on fire. They tried to extinguish the flames, and Emma was overcome by heat and smoke. Uncle Joe received some burns, but escaped. After the fire was put out, Emma's body was found in the charred debris of the living room about eight feet from where the front door had been. (*The St. Augustine Record*, June 23, 1955.) I remember seeing the smoke across the woods from my upstairs bedroom.

Telephones did not come to Sampson until after I married and left home in July 1958. Today's generation would be surprised to learn there was not only life before cell phones and I pods, but even before land line phones.

The building of I-95 through the middle of Sampson was the beginning of the end for the quiet rural community. Sampson was discovered as a location for development due to the new intersection of I-95 and 210, its beauty, and the fact that it was about halfway between St. Augustine and Jacksonville. Sampson resident Laura Mc Neil owned the property where the intersection of I-95 and 210 was to be. She was unwilling to sell her home and property, but eminent domain was enjoined, and she was forced to sell. The bulldozers were in her yard threatening to push the house over while she was still in it, forcing the widow to leave the old house with her young daughter. She then moved into a mobile home on the southeast side of I-95.

Mrs. Mc Neil was a former school teacher. She was sort of eccentric, but well loved in the community. She was the widow of Ferman Mc Neil, a grandson of Isador Ponce who was another early Sampson resident. Mrs. Mc Neil had a sister who used to sometimes come to Sampson and put up a screen in her yard to project movies for the enjoyment of the neighborhood.

After the government took Mrs. Mc Neil's home, she lived alone in a mobile home across the road from the truck stop that is now named T & A before there were two truck stops at 210 and I 95. One day a black man came to her door. She didn't recognize him, as there were no blacks living in the neighborhood. The man asked if he could have a glass of water. She told him to stay outside, and she would bring it to him. The man forced himself in, but didn't plan for the fact that Mrs. Mac Neil had a pistol in her hand under her apron. When he wouldn't leave, she shot and killed him. She was not charged, because the man had forced himself in and she had shot him in self-defense.

Before development, everyone knew everyone else in the rural community. Now there are the old-timers and the new-comers, and there is little mixing between the two groups. We don't share the same backgrounds and histories. The old-timers are overwhelmed by the growth and changes in our community and lifestyles, and the new-comers don't know we exist. It is so hard for us to realize that Sampson could ever have homes that sell for a half million dollars, many built on filled in ponds where once we hunted.

In the old parts of Sampson, family is so important that grandparents, children, and grandchildren live on adjacent properties. We look out for each other as generations of our families have always done. We have a closeness that it is impossible to find in the new developments where no family or history is shared among the residents. We know what country living really is, and it isn't living close enough to your neighbor that you can practically spit out of your window into his.

Sampson was a wholesome place for kids to grow up in the 1940s and 1950s. It was a place and time without televisions, telephones, and modern conveniences, but also without most of the opportunities that exist today for children to get into trouble. Drugs were unheard of. It was a community of families and friends who knew each other and where any adult could and would discipline any child with the appreciation of the child's parents. And woe unto the child who came home with a report from a teacher of some mischief or failure at school, because the punishment at home always exceeded that received at school. And yes, there was corporal punishment administered by teachers and the principal as well as by parents. Discipline was not a problem in schools during my childhood, because teachers were allowed to control their classrooms and parents upheld the teachers. No one even thought of suing the school board, the school, the principal, or the teacher for spanking a child, hitting his hand with a ruler, or humiliating him for some misdeed. Discipline worked!

School days were started with a prayer, a Bible reading, and saluting the flag. God was welcome. A picture of George Washington and the current president was in every high school class room. Teachers were patriotic and showed it. Americanism versus Communism was taught in high school. Current events were discussed. Kids were educated, and class disruption was not tolerated.

Sampson is where I learned to fish in the creek using a safety pin as a hook and a ball of bread for bait. It is where my father taught me to shoot and to squirrel hunt in Twelve Mile Swamp. It is where my mother taught me to sew and cook and about my religion; where my parents taught me the difference between good and evil, how to make do with what we had, manners, and many other things that have been useful throughout my life. In Sampson I met people who would remain life long friends and the boy who became the man I fell in love with and married and who became the father of my children.

It was a place where a child could breathe fresh country air; make use of his or her imagination; read a good book for entertainment or listen to "Roy Rogers", "Inner Sanctum", "Tom Mix", "The Grand Ole Opry" and other programs on the battery-operated radio. From Sampson, going to town was an exciting adventure, getting to see a Saturday movie was a rare and exciting experience, and a trip to Hilden to Mr. Roy Robinson's store called "The House that Jack Built" was a much looked-forward-to treat.

Mr. Roy's store had groceries, farm needs, animal feed, etc. No child ever went into his store without him giving them a Coca Cola, a package of Cracker Jacks or some treat that was rare to us country kids.

In Sampson many of the neighbors gathered with friends and relatives from town on Sundays for relaxation and entertainment, and we children could play with cousins and friends.

As children our parents took us to country dances at Switzerland, DuPont Center, Moccasin Branch or Mandarin and we were taught to dance by our parents. As teenagers we attended these dances with dates. The music was country (often called hillbilly) and by local bands that included a fiddle, guitar, and sometimes other instruments such as a bass fiddle, a washboard and even spoons. There was always a vocalist or two. We danced the two-step, fox-trot, jitterbug, Paul Jones, and the polka.

My early life in Sampson was by today's standards a life of deprivation and poverty, but it was from being creative with what we had and doing without the luxuries provided by electricity and other amenities that we later learned to value and appreciate running water, indoor plumbing, a hot tub of water in which to bathe, a home that is warm in winter and cool in summer, and all the modern conveniences that we enjoy today. Those who have never lived without them can't have the appreciation that those of us who grew up without them have.

Sampson was a place not appreciated nearly enough by me as a child, but looking back I am glad for having been raised in its country atmosphere. Living in Sampson helped to shape me into the person that I am and supplied me with experiences that I will never forget. As adults Yulee and I returned home to the place where we both grew up, and now I can appreciate all that it was, and I mourn for all that is missing from that more simple time and place. I am happy that our children were able to experience the area while it was undeveloped and natural. It is my hope and prayer that this article will educate people about the area, its former residents, its character, and its history, and that as Jacksonville meets St. Augustine, Sampson will never be forgotten or removed from the map to be replaced by some other name that has no historic connection. May it never be said that *once there was a place called Sampson.*

Sampson area (excerpted from the 1849 Survey of Township 5 South, Range 28 East of East Florida by R. W. Norris). This Sampson map shows the Peavelt/Peavett Grant which I 95 now crosses on its southeast corner. The roads below it meet at about the current intersection of 210 and 95 immediately north of F. J. Fatio's grant (shown). Except for Fatios Rd., they aren't named on this map. Russell Sampson Rd. approximately follows the northwestern extension of Fatios Rd. The eastern part went to Hilden. Above Fatios Rd. on the east a road follows the approx. route of 210 west of 95. Below the Peavett Grant and directly east of the square around 67, the home of P. Masters is shown. The square around 67 designates the 40 acres my parents bought in 1945.

Sampson from map on St. Johns County website. North is to the left of the page.

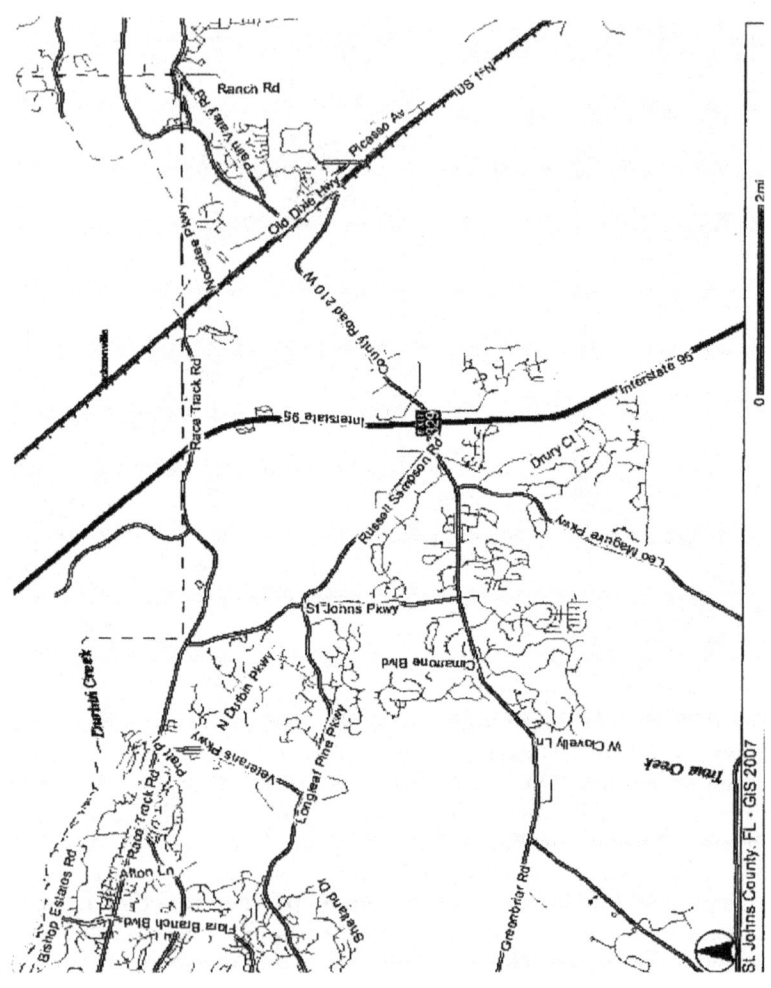

The Minorcans: They Came, They Suffered, They Conquered

While the 13 upper colonies were on the eve of declaring their independence from England, she planted another colony on the northeast coast of Florida. Shamefully, this later colony and its colonists have been ignored and forgotten by history.

When I was in grade school in the late 1940s, my teacher told each student to write a paper on where his or her ancestors were from and why they came to America. My maternal grandfather said a man named Turnbull brought his ancestors from a place called Minorca to New Smyrna, Florida. My teacher couldn't tell me any more about it than my grandfather. My encyclopedia made no mention of Turnbull, and my school library had no information to help me.

As I grew up, my family and many of our friends were referred to as Minorcans, but I didn't know whether to be proud or ashamed of the fact. Since then I have learned the Minorcan story, and I am proud to share the blood of this courageous group of people through three of my grandparents. I want my descendants to know their history also.

Because even a short time in the northeast Florida area will probably bring a person in contact with the word, if not in contact with an actual Minorcan, perhaps others would also like to know what and who a Minorcan is.

After the French and Indian War in 1763, Spain exchanged Florida for Havana, which England held. When the Spaniards left, the stage was set for the Minorcan colony. England encouraged the migration of people to Florida, because it intended them to be a market for

English goods, as well as producers of tropical crops and products for export to England.

A Scottish doctor, Andrew Turnbull, had a dream of owning a great plantation in Florida, worked by indentured Greek laborers. He and Sir William Duncan acquired 40,000 acres about 75 miles south of St. Augustine. Since Turnbull's wife was Greek, and she and their son had been born in Smyrna, Asia Minor, he named his colony New Smyrna for their birthplace.

Although Turnbull planned to populate his colony with Greeks, political conditions in Greece prevented his getting enough settlers there. He had chosen British-held Minorca, an island of the Balearic group in the Mediterranean Sea, as a place to gather colonists and supplies. After numerous trips to islands of the Mediterranean, he gathered 500 settlers, among them Greeks, Italians, and Corsicans which he brought to his base on Minorca.

According to E. P. Panagopoulos in *New Smyrna, an Eighteenth Century Greek Odyssey*, the colonists consisted of 100 Italians from Leghorn, Italy, and Greeks from Smyrna and Mani, Corona (a Greek port.). The Greeks were all young men who wanted peace and freedom from the Turks who had controlled Greece for more than 100 years. Other colonists were from the islands of the Agean Sea (part of the Mediterranean) and from Corsica.

While awaiting their departure for the New World on the isle of Minorca, many of the colonists married the Minorcan girls who were said to be beautiful, with fair skin, dark hair and flashing brown eyes. Three years of crop failure and these marriages prompted many Minorcans to ask to be taken to Florida also. Planning for 500 colonists, Turnbull found himself with nearly three times that many, almost two-thirds of them Minorcan.

The fact that most of the colonists were from Minorca led to all them being referred to as Minorcans, and to New Smyrna being called the Minorcan colony.

The Minorcans were gentle, Catholic people who had seen rough times and whose young women had married the colonists gathered by Turnbull on their island. They and the others agreed to go to New

Smyrna as indentured servants. At the end of their five to eight-year indentures, they were to be given their freedom and a plot of land.

Although England forbade Catholics in Florida, Turnbull allowed two Minorcan priests to come to the new colony, as the Minorcans would not leave without their spiritual leaders. One, Father Pedro de Campos, kept a register referred to as the *Golden Book of Minorcans*. In this book he kept the births, baptisms, marriages, and deaths of the colonists, and it is to him that we are indebted for most of what we know about these brave immigrants from across the sea.

Eight ships left Mahon, Minorca on March 31, 1768. Panagopoulos says, "This was a veritable achievement, because no one before had ever managed to bring so many people in one trip to colonize an American area."

One hundred and forty eight colonists died during the sea voyage which took more than three months. The more than 1,200 remaining settlers arrived in New Smyrna by the middle of summer, 1768.

In New Smyrna, Turnbull only had huts and provisions for 500 people. Matters would have been even worse for the colonists had an intended cargo of 500 slaves bound for the colony arrived, says Panagopoulos. Unfortunately, the ship wrecked off the coast and no slaves survived. As it was, food was scarce, because crops couldn't be planted until land was cleared. Indigo had to be planted where a swamp stood, and corn required dry land. Hominy grits, to be made from the corn, would be the main part of the colonists' diet for the nearly 10 years of the colony's survival.

Starvation was always a danger. Although the sea and streams abounded in fish, and the settlers were fishermen, they weren't given time to fish. Two years after the colony began, Panagopoulos says half of the colonists were dead from starvation, cruelty of the overlords who beat and abused them, and malaria from the relentless and savage mosquitoes.

In 1774, the colonists were accused of treason for being in contact with the Spanish in Havana. Some were harshly punished, according to Charlton W. Tebeau in *A History of Florida*, even though they were only trying to stay in contact with the nearest Catholic bishop who happened to be the Bishop of Cuba.

When the colony became successful financially, the treatment of the settlers didn't improve. They had to eat snakes, buzzards, alligators, even cowhide in order to survive.

Although the colony lasted almost 10 years, no one was ever given his freedom or any property, as promised, after the fulfillment of his contract. Almost 1,000 people died during this period. In June 1777, all the able-bodied settlers walked to St. Augustine, leaving Father Camps with those unable to walk the 75 miles. Governor Tonyn allowed the group to camp outside the city gates north of St. Augustine, and a few months later Father Camps joined them with the remaining Minorcans. This ended the colony of New Smyrna.

Turnbull's refusal to free the settlers from their completed indentures, his greed, his overseers' cruelty, the rigors of nature, personal differences between the new governor (Tonyn) and Turnbull, and the colonists' knowledge of the American Revolution in the upper colonies are cited by Panagopolous as reasons for the demise of the colony.

During the fall and winter of 1777, the city wall was the colonist's only shelter, and rain and cold took their toll. Governor Tonyn then granted them small plots in north St. Augustine. Panagopoulos says only 419 settlers remained in January 1778, and this figure includes the more than 100 children who had been born in New Smyrna.

When Florida was returned to Spain in 1783, nearly all the Minorcans stayed in St. Augustine. They had been separated from the British by religion, language and customs, and therefore welcomed the Spanish who were also Catholic and shared their culture.

Now, after 225 years since the ragged, starving group arrived in St. Augustine, many of their descendants still live in the area. Jane Quinn in *Minorcans in Florida* says there are approximately 3,500 with original names (although some are spelled differently) still in the vicinity. Many more have long since changed their names through marriage and cannot be counted.

The descendants of the colonists have made a considerable contribution to our history and culture. Among them are many who fought on both sides during the War Between the States and in all of our country's wars; two Catholic Bishops: Dominic Manucy and Anthony Domingo Pellicer; great American authors Steven Vincent Benet *(John Brown's Body)*, and William Rose Benet; and popular entertainers Judy and Diana Canova.

**North side of Old City Gates;
photo from Florida Memory Collection**

When one visits the nation's oldest city, travels the restored streets and looks back on history, it is largely the history of this group of people that one sees. Perhaps historians underestimate the importance of the colonists, if not the colony, in Florida's history. In St. Augustine, on the corner of St. George and Cathedral Streets, next to the Catholic Cathedral where Father Pedro de Camps is buried beneath the main altar, is the Minorcan Statue. It is a statue of Father Camps and a Minorcan family carrying a cross. On the base of the statue are engraved the names of the descendants of the Minorcan colonists who bear original settlers' names and still live in and near St. Augustine.

The Minorcan Statue; photo by author.

Other historic sites in St. Augustine are also testimony to the history of the colonists of the forgotten colony and their descendants. Among them are the Oldest House Museum where there is a tile mosaic of Governor Patrick Tonyn and a display dedicated to the Minorcans showing the cast net which was so important to their livelihoods; the Oldest Wooden Schoolhouse in America on St. George Street whose last roll call lists some of the same family names that are on the base of the Minorcan statue; the restored Fernandez Llambias House on St. Francis Street which was owned by several Minorcan families in the 1800s; and the Burgo Pellicer House, also on St. George Street, which is a reconstruction of the 1780s home of Francisco Pellicer and Jose' Peso de Burgo.

The Minorcans also contributed to the native cuisine. They are said to have brought the datil pepper to Florida, invented gopher turtle stew, and claim Minorcan clam chowder, Minorcan-style swamp cabbage, and according to Jane Quinn, even Mayonnaise, a sauce brought from Minorca and named after its capitol, Mahon - Mahonese sauce.

The Minorcans *was first published in* Florida Living, *Pages 15-17, September 1987, North Florida Publishing Co., Inc., 102 N.E. 10 Avenue, Suite 1, Gainesville, FL 32601, John Paul Jones, Jr., President and Publisher.*

When German-Dutch Protestants Met Minorcan Catholics

German/Dutch immigrants from Alsace, Lorraine, settled in Dutch Forks, South Carolina, around 1750. They had left their homes on the Germany/Holland border because of the anti-Protestant campaign of King Louis XIV. Among them was Peter Mickler (Michler, Miagler). The six Micklers who were the ancestors of all the Micklers who are long-time Floridians were Robert, James, Mahala, and Daniel Mickler, children of Peter and Lydia Allen Mickler III; and Jacob and William Mickler, sons of Jacob and Catherine Clark. The father of the first three was brother to the father of the other two. They were sons of Jacob Mickler and Eve (whose last name may have been Strum), and all five were the great-grandchildren of the first Peter Mickler.

The first to arrive in St. Augustine was Robert Mickler, about 1814, at age 14. He worked for an official of the Spanish regime, Antonio Jose Fernandez Mier. After Antonio's death, his widow, Ana Ortega (Ortagus) de Mier, married Robert Mickler. This was the first of the marriages between Mickler men and Minorcan women.

Robert's first cousin, Jacob, came to St. Augustine and married Manuela de Mier, daughter of Robert's wife, Ana and her first husband. This was the second Mickler- Minorcan marriage.

Other early Mickler-Minorcan unions were James Mickler and Mary Ann Arnau; William A. Mickler and Manuela Mickler (his first cousin, daughter of Jacob and Manuela), and after her death to another Minorcan lady, Josephine Reyes.

Daniel Mickler married Mary Ann Lowe in Camden County, and they moved to Suwanee County. Mary Ann was not of Minorcan descent.

Micklers have since united with other Minorcan families, among them the Pacetti, Pappy, Canova and Ponce families.

Many Micklers fought for the Confederacy and in the Indian Wars. One was a member of the Florida Legislature at the time of secession. Several surveyed the Everglades and for early railroads. A couple were St. Johns County Commissioners; one a St. Johns County sheriff. They were cattlemen (called Florida Crackers because of the sound made by the cow whips they used to control their herds), lumbermen, engineers, lawyers, boat captains, and farmers.

Manuela de Mier Mickler Dove

The Jacob and Manuela de Mier Mickler marriage produced 14 or 15 children, ten of whom lived to maturity. Five fought in the Civil War, and three gave their lives for the Confederacy. Their sons were well educated and prominent in St. John's County and the state. One daughter, Margaret, who married her first cousin, John (Mrs. J. H. Mickler), was a teacher. One of their daughters was Sister Julia Mickler who taught at St. Joseph's Academy for many years. Their descendants are plentiful in the area, and some are members of this parish.

The Micklers used the same names repeatedly for their progeny, making it confusing for those studying the family.

The early Florida Micklers were Protestant. Due to marriages to the lovely, Catholic women they came to love, some embraced the Catholic faith, and the children of all those who married the Minorcan women were baptized into the Catholic faith as babies. The religion that King Louis XIV could not force on their ancestors, some of these Micklers freely chose out of love for the beautiful, devout Minorcan women they had selected as brides, and the good examples these women provided. It is largely due to the faith of these Minorcan women who married the Protestant Micklers that the Diocese of St. Augustine and St. Joseph's Parish have long had Micklers as members.

This story was adapted from a story by the same name that was first published in St. Joseph's Reflections, *Vol. II, Issue 4, Christmas 1995, published by St. Joseph's Catholic Church, 11730 Old St. Augustine Rd., Jacksonville, FL 32258.*

Some Early Pioneers and the Loretto Parish

Around the turn of the century St. Joseph's Parish, referred to as the "Loretto Parish" by the Reverend P. J. Bresnahan in his book *Seeing Florida with a Priest*, included Diego (Palm Valley). Diego was on the circuit which the missionary Father Bresnahan visited, along with Bayard and Sampson, both of which are still within St. Joseph's Parish. Diego had a small Catholic chapel. Sampson had a Catholic Church or chapel and is even referred to on some older maps. There was no chapel in Bayard at that time, but Mass was held in the hall of Wing's Hotel, now occupied by the Bayard Country Store.

Widowed Yulee Mickler's second marriage, abt. 1904, was to the widow Barkoskie. This is part of their combined families. Each had 10 children from their previous marriages. Yulee is in back on the left wearing a hat.

Father Bresnahan describes a visit to Diego: "When I went there in December, 1905, it was a common hunting ground, especially for ducks, squirrels, turkeys, deer and wild hogs. Mr. Yulee Michler (sic) and family, with whom I put up, were, indeed, excessively kind and, I may add that, notwithstanding the difficulties they had to contend with, I never knew of better Catholics. In the course of time some of the children married non-Catholics, and without exception all these afterwards became zealous and fervent Catholics; another proof of the worth of good example on the part of parents.

"Besides the Michler family mentioned above, the other Catholics were the Miers and the Barkoskies, stepchildren of Mr. Michler . . . The sportsmen here, irrespective of creed, were bent on providing me with a good time of recreative hunting. I managed to get some ducks and squirrels as well as a good ducking in the swamp; for one of the Michler boys, volunteering to play horse for me in order to keep dry my clothes and shoes, and, with the help of a cow track and my weight, when half way across the swamp . . . succeeded in dumping me."

The Yulee Mickler that Father Bresnahan referred to had moved to Diego from St. Augustine about 1875. He was the youngest son of Jacob and Manuela de Mier Mickler. He and his wife, Susan Powers Mickler, had ten children. After her death in December 1900, he married the widow Barkoskie (Mary Lela Flynn) who also had ten children.

In his book, Father Bresnahan also discusses a mission in Sampson in January, 1907: "As Sampson was also attached to the Loretto parish I have an excuse . . . of telling of my visit to that strictly country district . . . . Marcus Papy, up to that period, only a nominal Catholic, gave me a bed to sleep in, fed me in the morning and evening, and good Tony Octagus [sic, should be Ortagus] saw to it that I got dinner, for which a pretty long walk each day whetted my appetite. I found Catholicity at a low ebb for various reasons, but I had an attendance of about forty every night, including about twenty practical Catholics. I prepared ten children for First Holy Communion, which they received in the local Catholic Chapel on the closing Sunday. That chapel has since disappeared. The faithful now residing in the district attend to their religious duties in the Chapel of Our Lady of Perpetual Help built in 1923 at Bayard by Rev. M. Fennell, the present pastor of Loretto . . . .

The nominal Catholics promised to do better, and I had the pleasure of bringing many to their duties before leaving. The local school teacher, Miss Henderson, was among the few applying for further instruction."

Marcus Pappy, abt. 1946

The Pappy family moved to Sampson between 1883 and 1892. Marcus' parents Joseph B. and Louisa Henry Papy and his brother Joseph L. Papy also resided in Sampson. Another brother, Robert, lived in the San Jose area and owned Pappy's guava jelly factory. However the Pappys who are members of St. Joseph's are descendants of Marcus.

Some of the Micklers of St. Joseph's are descendants of Yulee Mickler and others are not, but all are related. Some other old local families related by marriage to the Micklers are Hartley, Losco, Rogero, and, of course, Pappy. The Pappys are also related by marriage to many older families, including Hartley, Roache, Ponce, Pacetti, and Danese.

The Micklers and Pappys have been associated with St. Joseph's from almost its very beginning and are very much a part of its history.

"Some Early Pioneers and the Loretto Parish" *was first published in* St. Joseph's Reflections, *Vol. III, Issue 1, Easter 1996, published by St. Joseph's Catholic Church, 11730 Old St. Augustine Rd., Jacksonville, FL 32258. It has been edited and updated here.*

Confederate Scout William A. Mickler

The Florida paper *DIXIE* carried an article in 1915 which started with an excellent introduction for the story of the brave and daring Confederate scout, William Alfred Mickler:

> Search the records of civil strife from its beginning in 1861 to its ending in 1865, and you will find no more interesting incidents in the development of the raw civilian into the perfect type of soldier than in the career of Captain William Mickler.

William was only 21 when he enlisted in the Confederate Army in Grahamville, South Carolina, He was the youngest of three brothers who enlisted together. He and his brother, Huger, were both attached to Wade Hampton's 2nd South Carolina Cavalry, Company B. They were the sons of William A. Mickler Sr. and his wife Mahala Mickler, first cousins, of Bluffton, South Carolina. William Sr. was a blacksmith.

William was born in Bluffton, South Carolina on April 23, 1840. He was the fifth of eight children. Huger J. Mickler was the fourth child in the family. The third in the trio of brothers who were Confederate scouts was John Henry Mickler, the eldest child, born about 1832. John and Huger were educated at the Citadel in South Carolina. They were there on scholarship.

William was only 21 when he enlisted, and was quickly promoted to Corporal and then to Sergeant. He fought in the battles of Williamsburg, Seven Pines, Antietam, Chancellorsville, and Gettysburg.

General Wade Hampton's first scouting party was commanded by William Mickler in 1861. He started with four men, but later led a detail from each company in the regiment which included 18 or 19 men. One of the men was his brother Huger.

They had only pistols and swords as weapons, but soon their pistols were all pairs of Union Colts gained from the enemy.

Mickler's mission was to keep the Prince William County, Virginia, roads and lanes free of Yankees. This area was also patrolled by Union scouts to keep the Confederates out, leading to frequent small wars between the opposing groups of scouts.

A favorite trick of Mickler's was hiding in the pines. Once he and his group of five scouts got within a hundred or so yards of eight or ten Yankees on the Brentsville Street undetected while in the pines. They killed five and captured the rest. Sgt. Mickler claimed to have killed the Yankee in charge, Sgt. Redmond, who begged Mickler to take care of his horse George before he breathed his last. The horse was renamed Redmond in his former master's honor and Mickler rode it until it died.

Sgt. Mickler hid his scouts in the pines on the bank of the run near Greenwood Church when they spotted a regiment of Yankee scouts. The Yankees rode in to water their horses, and Mickler ordered his men to fire. The Union horses stampeded and Mickler ordered his men to charge. They ran the enemy to its picket lines near Dumfries. When they returned with their prisoners, all the enemy along the route were dead or wounded.

It was during a mission near Greenwood Church that Sgt. Mickler's beloved brother Huger was killed. The following is an excerpt from E. Prioleau Henderson's *Autobiography of Arab*.

> A short time after this, Sergt. Mickler was preparing to make a scout down in the "Forest." He ordered Corpl. Huger Mickler to take George Crafton and a Virginia scout, named Pierson, and go down the day before and find out the different picket posts of the enemy; also a reserve picket post he had heard of near Dumfries. After accomplishing this work, he would find him (the Sergeant) at Smith's house, near Old Bacon Race Church, the following night. Corpl. Mickler got ready and rode over where his brother and my master were staying to get his final instructions. I

remember how handsome he looked that afternoon and how nicely he was dressed, in his new grey uniform, new hat, boots and gauntlets, all captured ready-made from the enemy, except the cloth, from which his Virginia sweetheart had made the suit. . . . I had always liked and admired the Corporal, for . . . I always liked brave men. Poor fellow, six hours later he was a corpse, literally riddled with Yankee bullets.

The sergeant soon followed the three scouts down with his entire party, and stopped as agreed upon at Smith's house to await the coming of his brother. I heard my master say afterwards, that he and Mickler had retired for the night, leaving word with Smith to call him when his brother arrived. He said, before they got to sleep, they heard a knock at the door, sergt. Mickler sprung from the bed and asked, "Is that you, Huger?" A voice answered, "No, sergeant, it is I, George Crafton. I have sad news to tell you about poor Huger. He is killed." My master says the Serge[a]nt fell like he was shot - for they loved each other very dearly, those two brothers. Crafton entered the room and told them the particulars of his death. Said the three of them were riding abreast near Greenwood Church, where they intended riding their horses in the pines and "taking it a foot," when they rode into an ambuscade of the enemy, who without even halting them, fired a volley on them, killing Corpl. Mickler. George Crafton and Pierson escaped by a miracle, their clothing being perforated in several places. Pierson had two bullet holes through his hat, besides those through his coat. Fortunately neither of their horses were hit, so they escaped, leaving their comrade's body "in the hands of the enemy." The Yankees the next day established a picket post at the church. They kindly allowed the citizens to bury Corpl. Mickler's body, and the remains of the gallant Corpl. Huger Mickler still rest in old Greenwood Church-yard.

Corporal Huger J. Mickler died in July, 1861.

William and E. Prioleau Henderson (author of *Autobiography of Arab*), also from the Beaufort District Troop were among nine men from that troop chosen by J. E. B. Stuart, Commander of the Southern Cavalry, to make raids far into the north. Only the best riders and most capable soldiers were chosen by Stuart for this important mission.

Mickler and the other scouts captured 750 horses for General Lee's artillery in Stuart's three-day raid on Chambersburg in June 1862. Lee's artillery was desperately in need of horses, and this was considered one of Stuart's most successful raids. The scouts destroyed property and collected horses while crossing and re-crossing the Potomac in sight of Washington, D.C.

In November 1862, Mickler and his scouts assisted in the capture and bringing in of most of General Burnside's Christmas supplies.

One feat that characterized the heroic soldier was a brave and daring rescue of Private Eldred Simpkins at the Barber's Cross Roads fight in early 1863. Private Simpkins of Mickler's company fell and was pinned under his horse when it was shot by the enemy. Sgt. Mickler rode back to him, jumped off his horse, freed the Private, and took him up behind his own horse as the enemy was about to capture them.

The 1st Michigan Cavalry, who had been made aware of the well-known and effective scouts, threatened to "eat them up without salt." A different scenario developed when a detachment of the Michigan Cavalry actually met up with Mickler's band. The born woodsman and scout with only three of his men against ten of their riflemen, made mincemeat of them. Three were immediately shot; the rest fled, but were followed by Mickler and his men. Two were shot, four captured, and finally, the lieutenant in command was taken when his horse refused to jump a fence. Neither Mickler nor his scouts were harmed.

Mickler obtained information from the Yankee lieutenant that several companies of the 1st Michigan were in Brentsville and soon would return. Mickler left the wounded men and prisoners with a few of his men (there were 17 in all at the time), and planned an ambush with the rest. Finding a place in the embankment where the road cut through a hill, he strung the men out in the trees. After the passing of the advance scouts, Mickler and his men fired on the head of the column. Mayhem followed as men and horses fell and others tried to ride over them. Once again the Yankees were chased to their picket lines, while men and horses were captured along the way. Only one of Mickler's men was seriously wounded. Several Yankees were killed, many wounded, and many taken prisoner. It was during this raid that Mickler's captured horse Redmond died. The 1st Michigan on second thought must have wished it could have avoided a taste of Mickler and his scouts – with or without salt!

An Extract from General Orders No. 29, Headquarters, Army of Northern Virginia, 28th February, 1863, obviously referred to this battle.

> A detachment of seventeen men of Hampton's Brigade, under the brave Sergt. Mickler, attacked and scouted a body of forty-five Federals near Wolf Run Shoals, killing and wounding several, and bringing off fifteen prisoners, with the loss of our part of Sergt. Sparks, of the 2nd. S.C. Regiment.
> By Command of General Lee
> (signed R. H. Chilton
> A.A. Ils, General)

According to the book *Autobiography of Arab*, Sparks, though critically wounded, did not die in this attack.

The Union Army dispatched a crack regiment, the 8th Illinois Cavalry led by Col. Fonsworth to break up, capture, and drive Mickler's band out of Prince William County, Virginia.

It seemed the whole Yankee army eventually knew about Mickler and his scouts, and they were all chasing him. Things got too hot for Mickler and company in Prince William County, Virginia. They were forced to cross the Blue Ridge Mountains, and there joined John S. Mosby's troops.

On June 8, 1863, Robert E. Lee reviewed J. E. B. Stuart's ten thousand man cavalry at Brandy Station. Mickler and his scouts were among the ten thousand. The encampment was attacked early next morning by Federal troops in the largest cavalry battle of the War Between the States. It was the first battle in which the South was not victorious. The battle, in fact, was a draw. Hampton's Brigade bore the brunt of the fighting for some time in this fight. The Cavalry fought hand-to-hand combat.

Mickler and his small band of scouts marched with General Stuart towards Pennsylvania soon after. They engaged in many raids during the Gettysburg Campaign and participated in the Battle of Gettysburg.

Major General J. E. B. Stuart wrote the Secretary of War a note to accompany the request for Mickler's promotion on September 25, 1863.

> Respectfully forwarded and strongly recommend for promotion on account of conspicuous gallantry and valuable services . . .

Lieutenant Colonel T. J. Lipscomb also recommended his promotion:

> I have the honor to recommend St. William A. Mickler, for 2nd. Lieut. . . . Sergt. Mickler has distinguished himself upon several occasions and has been of much service as a scout.

Sgt. Mickler had been appointed the rank of 2nd. Lieutenant on October 19, 1863. This rank was confirmed in January of 1864 and he was given command of another band of scouts. This time they operated between the northern forces and Wilmington on the Cape Fear River.

In December 1863, while checking on Federal Army movements, Sgt. Mickler stopped at the home of the Widow Burdine, a northern settler. Her niece warned Mickler that her aunt had three Yankee officers hidden in her cellar. Mickler and another scout raised the cellar door, and as he stepped on the first step, the Yankees shot him, shattering his leg below the knee. Mickler could not return to duty until March 1864. His wound bothered him for the rest of his life. According to Henderson's book, Sgt. Sparks had just returned to duty following his serious wound, and it was during this episode that Sparks was killed.

In the spring of 1864, Mickler's Regiment was ordered back to South Carolina. Only fourteen of the eighty-six who had enlisted returned. Most of the missing were dead. Mickler found his family home had been burned down during the burning of Bluffton on June 4, 1863. The location of the home was at the end of present-day Colcock St. on the May River.

In June of 1864, War Records show that Lt. Mickler attempted to resign his position as 1st. Lieutenant, proving he had been promoted again in that short period of time.

> Camp 2nd. Reg T, S.C. Cav.
> Green Pond, S.C.
> June 15th, 1864
>
> To the Hon. James Seddon, Sec'y of War,
> I have the honor to send in my resignation upon the condition that I be transferred for duty as a scout to Virginia to report to Maj. Gen'l Wade Hampton. For a long time previous to my regiment being transferred to this dep't., I was engaged in scouting in Virginia, and I make this application with the belief that I can render more efficient service to my country in that capacity than in my present position.
>
> Very respectively,
> William A. Mickler
> 1st Lieut., Co. B, 2 SC Cav.

Colonel Lipscomb responded:

> Respectfully approve. Lieut. Mickler is a good and worthy officer, and I concur with him in the belief that he would be more essential as a scout than in his present command.

When Lt. Mickler's letter was referred to General Hampton to see if his services as a scout were desire, the General replied:

> I recommend that Lt. Mickler be allowed to come on, returning to his work. He is an admirable scout and if placed in command of a part would do good service.

Something major must have occurred which caused the lieutenant to have second thoughts, because two weeks later, on June 30, he again wrote to Secretary of War Seddon:

> I had the honor of transmitting to you some days ago, my conditional resignation, the condition being that I should be transferred to Gen'l. Hampton's command as a scout.

Since that time circumstances have occurred to render it imperative that I should stay with my command, and I must respectfully beg leave to withdraw my resignation.

The brave scout evidently felt his talents were being wasted, because on December 16, 1864, he again wrote the Secretary of War.

> Sir:
> I have the honor to tender my resignation as 1st. Lieut. of Company "B" 2nd. So. Ca. Cavalry. My reasons for doing so are that the enemy now are in the section of South Carolina in which I was residing at the commencement of the war, and I am thoroughly acquainted with that section of the country. Believing that I can be of a great deal more service to my country in the capacity of a scout than in my present position, I respectfully ask to report to Brig. Gen'l. P. M. B. Young in So. Ca. as a scout having been scouting for Gen'ls. Young and Hampton for two years previous to my promotion.

On January 10, 1865, his resignation as 1st Lieutenant of Company B., 2nd. Regiment, was accepted, and in February 1865, William Mickler was promoted to Captain. He was reunited with his brother Captain John Mickler. Both scouted for Gen. P. M. B. Young until the end of the war when they were paroled by the General on April 16, 1865, at the end of the war.

> When the scouts reported in a 'body' at Augusta, Georgia, to be paroled by Gen. Young the 16th day of April, 1865 . . . after all the scouts had received their paroles, they mounted their horses to leave the Gen'ls. Headquarters, when he called the Micklers and [Henderson] back, when the 3 scouts entered the house, they were looking very sad; but when they came out, after a parting hand-shake with the General on the steps, they all three looked 'very smiling.' And I, Arab, . . . concluded – yes, the General had been giving them some of that medicine. (*Autobiography of Arab*)

Near the end of the war while they were scouting in the path of General Sherman's destruction, the Mickler brothers observed the bands of freed slaves. They were killing their former masters, stealing from the helpless women and children, and causing havoc and creating mischief. Following the war, they joined a band of vigilantes to protect old men, women, and children from the pillage and outrage committed by the former slaves. They were labeled "guerrillas" by the government and were outlawed for their activities. The Mickler brothers were forced to flee to South Florida with a $10,000 price on their heads.

William married his first cousin, Manuella Mickler before 1870. She was the daughter of William's paternal Uncle Jacob. John Mickler married Manuella's sister Margaret. In 1870, the two brothers and their wives were living outside St. Augustine, in Sampson, St. Johns County, Florida. In 1880, William and Manuella were living in Sampson and with them was their daughter Jessie and Manuella's mother, also Manuella Mickler Dove.

William's first wife died in 1883. They were the parents of two daughters, Maria Jessie (known as Jessie) Mickler (1872-1935), and Mary Theresa Mickler (1874-1884). Jessie married Henry C. Price.

William married again in 1884 to Josephine Margaret Reyes. They lived in Sampson for a time, as well as in St. Augustine. Eventually they settled at the head of the North River in Palm Valley, Florida. They were the parents of eleven children: Hugo Camilla Mickler (1885-1900); William Germaine/Felix Mickler (1887-1956) [my grandfather]; Frances Jane Mickler (1888 - 1984); Marie J. Mickler (1888-?); Anne E. Mickler (1889-1987); Wade Hampton Mickler (1891-1909); Emma Frances Mickler (1891-1998); Florida Mickler (1894-1904); Belle Catherine Mickler (1894-1975); Rosa M. Mickler (1896-1990); and Cecelia Josephine Mickler (1898-1994).

William applied for a Confederate Soldier's Pension in 1901, and was granted a pension of $120 a year.

State of Florida, St. Johns County
14th Feb 1901

(carefully and fully the facts surrounding the injury) Scouting scout sent by Gen. Wade Hampton (the character and especially the extent of the

injury and disability resulting therefrom) I was shot by the federalists between the ankle and knee and my leg broken.

William Alfred Mickler,
ca. 1907

We, the undersigned physicians, residents of the State and county aforesaid, do solemnly attest that we have carefully examined William A. Mickler, who is personally known to us to be the person above applying for a pension under the laws of Florida and find he is suffering the result of a gunshot wound in left leg. The bone was badly fractured. The result is the leg is unset and assumes a rheumatis form rendering walking both painful and difficult and by reason of the wound received he is unable to gain a living by manual labor which is his only means of support for himself and family. We know the above to be true by seeing him from time to time on our streets and at his home. We have no interests in this claim or are related to the party.

16th Feb 1901 signed by Dr. Rainey, M.D., St. Augustine, Florida and Wm. F. Shine, M.D., St. Augustine, Florida State

According to the newspaper article published in *DIXIE* in 1915, William was at one time a St. Johns County Commissioner. In 1907, William A. Mickler was Sergeant-at-arms of the Florida Legislature. He died in St. Johns County, Florida, September 7, 1916, and was buried in San Lorenzo Catholic Cemetery. Josephine Reyes Mickler, his wife, died in St. Augustine, Florida, October 19, 1927.

William Mickler's daughter, my Great-aunt Emma, told the following to me in 1987:

> Papa joined the Confederate Army in South Carolina. His father was a blacksmith in Bluffton, South Carolina, Papa's home. A rich man gave Papa a horse so he could join the cavalry.

> Papa talked about Prioleau (E. P. Henderson) all the time. He didn't know Prioleau had written a book until it came out and his sister sent a copy to him from South Carolina. He was so proud of it. He said he would have added some to it if he'd been asked.

Papa used to tell about his Yankee girl friends. He said the Yankee girls were real nice to him. In fact, two of them were so nice, he named two of us after them (she didn't say which two).

Papa and his brother, Uncle John and some others were part of an organization in South Carolina that protected women and children from bands of freed slaves. For his activities the Federal Government put a price on his head. He had to hide out in South Florida for a while. Then he went to St. Augustine where he married his first cousin. She died after fifteen years of marriage, and a couple of years later he married Mama. He was forty-five, she was twenty-five.

What I remember most about Papa is how loving he was. He was very proud of his children and Uncle John's daughter Sister Julia (a Roman Catholic Nun.) He was a true gentleman and insisted men treat women like ladies.

Papa talked about the war all the time. He was proud of his part in it. I wish I had paid more attention when he talked about it. I was too young to realize I'd want to know about it someday and he wouldn't be here to tell me. He died when I was twenty-eight, you know. He knew people would be interested someday. He would have loved for someone to interview him about it.

Aunt Emma was instrumental in having the William A. Mickler Chapter of the United Daughters of the Confederacy chartered in St. Augustine, Florida, in July 1982. It began with 51 members. This was a lifelong dream of Aunt Emma's.

Bibliography:

Confederate Service Record. 2nd. S.C. cavalry, Roll 12.
DIXIE, Jacksonville, Florida, July 31, 1915.
Henderson, E. Prioleau. *Autobiography of Arab*.
Walter, John F. "Personalized History of William A. Mickler.
Mickler, Patricia Ferguson. *The Micklers of Florida*.
Mickler, Latrell E. "William A. Mickler, Confederate Scout". *The United Daughters of the Confederacy Magazine*, Vol LI, No. 1. January 1988.

One Heroic Catholic Family

She was a few days shy of her ninth birthday, alone on a train that would take her from her home in Nebraska to St. Mary's orphanage in Jacksonville, Florida. Tears streamed from her eyes as she looked at the apple in her hand, her only possession except for the clothes she wore. Her family had lost everything after her father, a cavalry soldier in the U.S. Army whose outfit fought next to Teddy Roosevelt's Rough Riders in Cuba during the Spanish American War, died as the result of an injury sustained while in the army. Now destitute, her mother could no longer care for her, and she was heartbroken and scared.

Maude Newman, her brother Everett, her mother Martha Mizell Newman, and her brother James, abt 1904, Washington, D.C.

Maude Elizabeth Newman had been born in Washington, D. C., on May 21, 1901, into a happy home. She had an older and a younger brother. The family was sound financially until health problems caused by her father's unfortunate accident dwindled away their small fortune on costly medical care. He reportedly fell from his horse while training horses for the army, and severely injured his back.

Maude's mother Martha had accompanied her father James Newman to Savannah, Georgia, in order to care for him, leaving her two oldest children in Fanning, Scotts Bluff, Nebraska, in the care of James' brother Edwin and his wife. James died in a Savannah Hospital on November 7, 1908.

Maude was to later tell her children the reason she was abruptly sent to Jacksonville was because she had seen her aunt kissing a man while her Uncle Edwin was away on business. This made her aunt angry, and she was probably also scared that Maude would tell her uncle.

The 1910 census lists Maude and her brother in Fanning, Nebraska on May 7, 1910, and in the home of her mother in Jacksonville, Florida, on May 14, 1910; perhaps when their aunt telegrammed their mother that Maude was on the train, Martha demanded that Everett be put on the next train.

Martha, destitute, had to work. She paid the orphanage to care for Maude.

Maude arrived at St. Mary's home about May of 1910, a very frightened, lonely creature, one among many others. Although the nuns who raised her scrupulously cared for the physical and religious needs of their charges, they could not replace the loving home and family she missed so much.

The environment was strict and regimental. The children, like the nuns, were not allowed any personal belongings, sharing even the clothes they wore. Maude was immediately given responsibilities, including the care of the younger children whom she loved and for whom she had such sympathy.

She lived there about seven years. At age 16 she married Raymond Yulee Mickler on July 3, 1917. He was a widower 20 years her senior, and is described by all who knew him as a saintly man who was a wonderful husband and father, a hard worker, and a good provider, as well as a devout Catholic. One of the first things he did after their marriage was to surprise his bride by bringing her younger brother James from St. Leo's Orphanage in Tampa to their home on Pearl Street in Jacksonville to live with them.

From the beginning they welcomed needy children and adults into their home. As the family grew they moved to Mandarin, then to Sampson, which their younger children recall when they think of home.

Maude began keeping children from St. Mary's Orphanage about 1920. In 1940, when Kathleen Riley was sent to Jacksonville to start Catholic Charities of Florida, Maude told her she would take all the orphans who needed a home. Her unhappy life without family resulted in her desire to rescue as many children as she could from life in an orphanage, and to give them the loving family she had so longed for.

Raymond Y. Mickler (1879-1955)

She and Raymond became the parents of 12 children of their own, one who died as a toddler. Their foster children were treated exactly as their own children, who helped Maude, according to their age and abilities, with the many tasks such great responsibilities entailed. Raymond provided for and loved them all.

In 1953, while the family lived in Sampson on 38 acres, complete with fruit trees, chickens and livestock, and lots of outdoors for happy children, 24 people were living in the Mickler home. That year, Maude was honored as Catholic Boarding Mother of the Year.

After Raymond's death in 1955, Maude, again in Mandarin, continued to care for children, mostly babies, until her untimely death, the result of a traffic accident, on August 22, 1967.

Surely the Holy Spirit worked in the lives of Maude and Raymond to transform unhappy and tragic pasts into loving, sharing, and giving lives that were beneficial, not just to their own family, but to so many others. It is estimated they cared for over 500 foster children. What a wonderful example of a heroic Catholic family they became.

Raymond, you see, was also the victim of a terrible tragedy. His first wife had died in childbirth, and is said to be buried with her twins, one in each arm.

One Heroic Catholic Family *was previously published in* St. Joseph's Reflections, *page 23, Summer, 1999 Issue, St. Joseph's Catholic Church, 11730 Old St. Augustine Rd., Jacksonville, FL 32258, Publisher.* I have expanded the earlier version here.

Bobwhite Quail Hunting: Not what it Used to Be

"When I was a boy, it was nothing to kill 100 bobwhites before noon," my Daddy told me more than once; he filled orders for the St. Augustine market in the 1920s. The picture Daddy painted in my mind of the Florida landscape of that time helps to explain why Florida's quail hunting has so drastically changed. At that time cattle roamed free in the woods, and the cattle owners kept the underbrush burned to make forage better. This made ideal quail habitat. Civilization had not yet encroached, and where the few residents of Sampson lived, there were farms and fields, also contributing to the flourishing of quail; the bobwhite's southern range had not yet been largely converted to giant pine plantations. It is because of the change in most of the former quail habitat due to timber growing, the lack of controlled burning, the large housing developments in once rural areas, and the fact that the wildlife officials are not managing public lands for quail, that hunting the bobwhite quail in the south isn't what it used to be, and has completely disappeared in many areas.

Terrell Pappy with bird dog and quail

Florida and other southern states' game management departments are primarily interested in managing for deer populations, with turkeys being second on the agenda. The same goes for most private hunting clubs.

If a hunter can afford to hunt where pen-raised quail are released in open fields, or if he has access to some private farmlands, he may not be affected by the changes. However, many hunters have but two choices - hunt on public-owned land or on type II management areas which are usually owned by timber companies which allow the public to hunt their properties. Even public lands host tree plantations, making bobwhite hunting conditions much the same for either option.

These hunters know that even if they locate a covey, chances are they will not take more than two or three birds on a covey rise - and they'll feel lucky to get any. It is only the love of the sport that sends these die-hards back to try again.

When pines are planted, they are usually arranged in neat rows and are grown as thick as possible in order to get maximum yield per acres. Clear cuts are usually scattered among the planted pines. These clear cuts that have reached the stage of seed-bearing weeds provide forage for quail. It is in these places that today's bobwhite quail hunter and his dog hunt in hopes of locating a covey.

The problem with hunting pine plantations (and another reason quail hunting isn't what it used to be) is the lack of large areas sparsely populated with trees. The old fields, large areas burned by cattle owners, and most of the black-jack ridges of yesteryear are gone. When a dog points a covey and the hunter flushes it, the covey immediately flies into the adjacent planted pines. Unless the hunter can line the bird up between the rows, he may as well forget it. It's nearly impossible to shoot birds when there are trees every few feet, especially when there is also neck-high brush such as palmettos and gall berry bushes.

Back in the middle of the century yearly burning of the forests fell into disfavor. Reforestation, the planting of pine trees, was the reason for the cessation of burning the woods. Cattle owners' reasons for burning were to eliminate the brush and get a fresh crop of tender, green shoots to feed cattle, and to destroy the ticks that flourished in the brush.

For a while in the 1980s it seemed that controlled burning of the woods was coming back into favor with foresters as a natural and cheap method of eliminating devastating forest fires, controlling tree diseases, and returning nutrients to the soil. That was good news to hunters, because the practice is beneficial to quail and other wildlife, allowing new growth that produces seed-bearing weeds, and areas for scratching for worms, insects and roots. The elimination of the underbrush also makes it easier for bobwhite hunters to see their dog, and the quail when they are flushed.

Unfortunately more plantations will not adopt this practice in spite of the fact that it is the best management tool. Population growth into rural areas, more cars on the roads, and more roads are the reasons. Smoke settling on the highways causes accidents. Accidents draw lawyers. Lawyers file lawsuits. Now in favor are judges and juries that award victims and families huge damages, which threaten to bankrupt the property owners and force government to deny burn permits. Environmentalists, too, file lawsuits, claiming the smoke causes health problems. But the results of not burning are often costly, too, and every year more acres of timber, private and public, are lost to devastating fires that could have been prevented by controlled burning; every year whole communities of homes are lost that need not have been. Every year property and home insurance prices rise.

Unless environmentalists, the government, and the general public again realize the benefits of controlled burning as a way to prevent the devastation caused by wildfires that are impossible to control; the benefits that controlled burning brings in helping control lymes and other tick-borne disease; and the benefits of controlled burning to wildlife (which everyone claims to love); quail populations will not increase, nor will the hunter's chances to bag his limit. In fact, the quail will join other forms of wildlife on the threatened, and possibly, endangered wildlife list.

Bobwhite quail are found in more than half the states in our country. They range as far north as Maine, as far south as Florida, and as far west as South Dakota. And even though bobwhite hunting has changed considerably since Daddy's day, along with quail, die hard quail hunters still exist. Although bobwhite quail hunting may never again be what it was in the 1920s, it does offer a challenge that only a special kind of person can appreciate. That person is a hunter who isn't after an easy kill, but one who enjoys the companionship and cooperation of a good dog, the peace and seclusion of the woods, and the *sport* of bobwhite hunting. A few quail for the table is just an added bonus. *(This is a previously unpublished article written in 1986)*

Daddy's Bargain

As we turned off the dirt road and pulled up to a picket fence, Daddy said, "Well, this is it."

I was six, but I can see it now. I burst into tears, because behind the weathered gray fence stood a two-story house, just as gray and weathered, with a porch that sagged around three sides of it.

The house was surrounded by huge live oaks with moss hanging like gray beards from their limbs. Everything was gray except the large, white sand yard, which had been raked clean.

It looked like a rickety, haunted house in the middle of an immense, bare dessert, except for those giant oaks which hovered over all.

Mama, Daddy, my little sister and I cautiously picked our way up the broken steps and across the dilapidated porch to the front door. It had no lock, and as Daddy pushed it open, we peered into a room that had never been finished, even though the house was seventy-five years old. (I learned this a few years later when we were playing in front one afternoon, as a car with two old ladies drove up to the picket fence. One said their father, a Mr. Salas, had built that house in about 1870, and they just wanted to see if it was still there.)

The walls had cracks between the boards that daylight peeped through; so did the ceiling, which was the floor of an upstairs bedroom. Cobwebs were in every corner, some with huge spiders, and roaches scampered across the floor.

I cried louder, and my little sister wrapped her arms around Mama's legs, fright apparent in her wide eyes.

Daddy led the way through a doorway on the right side into the other downstairs room, the kitchen. It was then I noticed there were no electric lights.

The kitchen was large, with cabinets of the same unfinished wood on one wall. There was no sink, but a small, black iron wood stove with enamel trim stood between the back door and a window. This room was in no better condition than the first.

In a corner of the kitchen, a narrow, steep staircase went up four steps before turning and disappearing around a corner. A small closet stood behind a door under the stairs.

At the top of the stairs was a blank wall with a door on each side. The door on the left was open. The room seemed large, with two single hung windows on the front wall overlooking a patched porch roof. A smaller window was high in the wall by the corner nearest the stairs. I could only see up into oak limbs and moss when I looked out of it. This room had its share of cobwebs and roaches also. Daddy announced that this was to be his and Mama's room.

None of us were ready for what faced us when Daddy flung the door open so we could examine the last room. Chickens squawked and flew out of the two largest windows overlooking the equally patched rear porch! These windows had no glass; they were just holes in the wall.

The floor had an old rug covering it. The rug was so deep in chicken droppings that the color was no longer discernable. I suppose the rug saved the kitchen from the droppings, some of which would have fallen through the floor cracks. The odor was terrible, a thick mixture of mildew, dust, and chicken waste, causing me to have a sneezing fit.

Another window like the high one in the other bedroom was on the same side of the house as that one. It had a glass. The opposite wall also had a window larger than the small one, but much smaller than the gaping holes in the rear wall. This one had a wooden shutter that opened to the outside instead of a glass.

Even my brave Mama was in tears by now, which caused wailing from my little sister.

The year was 1945; the month was October. World War II was barely over. Times were hard, and Daddy had bought a bargain - forty acres came with the house, and he bought it all for $300.

Mama, with the help of other ladies in the rural neighborhood, spent the rest of the day scrubbing the living room with bleach and water that they had to draw from a well in the back yard. That night our beds were set up in the living room. We slept there every night for a week while Mama scrubbed the rest of the house until she felt it was sanitary enough for our use.

She nailed canvas hammocks someone had given her to the tops of the window holes in our bedroom, and these were rolled up on old broom handles to let in light. At night they were let down to keep out some of the bloodthirsty mosquitoes. Not a door or window in the house had a screen.

The house also had no bathroom. An outhouse, a one-holer, stood a hundred or so feet from the house, behind a grapevine. Baths were taken in the kitchen in a number three washtub. Water had to be drawn from the well, carried to the kitchen, and heated, so we all used the same water. I loved it when I was first and the water was hot and fresh, but often begged off when I was to be last. I never trusted that my little sister didn't wee- wee in the bath water.

Before moving here we had lived in the Riverside area of Jacksonville, in a garage apartment belonging to Daddy's boss. We had electricity, indoor plumbing, a snug and cozy apartment, and close neighbors. Now we lived in the woods in a community called Sampson. We were half a mile from our nearest neighbors and twenty miles from the nearest town, St. Augustine.

Previously I had been driven to and from a private school (I had just started primer class); here I rode a bus three hours a day roundtrip, to and from a four-class room, eight grade country school, Mill Creek.

How I hated that ugly, uncomfortable house! Wind whipped through the cracks in winter. When it rained we slept with canvas over the blankets to keep the roof from leaking on us. In winter we slept under stacks of quilts so thick it was difficult to turn over. When one of is did - my sister shared the bed with me - the other came uncovered.

The only heat was from the wood stove in the kitchen. Mama, God bless her, would get up at 4:00 in the morning to start a fire so we could jump up, grab the clothes we had lain out the night before, and go down to the warm kitchen to dress in comfort.

In summer, scorpions would fall from the rafters and sting us with their curled tails if we dated to brush them off when we felt them crawl on us. Dirt dauber wasps carried black widow spiders to their mud homes in the rafters, also. Occasionally their paralyzed bodies would fall or be dropped on our bed.

The nearby creek was our laundry. On Saturdays we would get up early, strip the beds, and Daddy would carry the laundry in the car a quarter mile behind the house to Sampson Branch. When the sun got warm, Mama would pack a picnic basket, and we would walk to the creek where she actually washed our clothes for several years.

My sister and I loved washday in summer, because we played in the shallow water of the white bottomed creek while mama scrubbed clothes on the washboard. In the middle of the day we would eat whatever goodies Mama had packed in the basket. When all the clothes were washed, we would spread them on bushes to dry. Late in the afternoon Daddy would go to the creek and bring the clothes back in the car.

In spite of the ugliness of the house, and all the misery and inconvenience we suffered, it wasn't long before I loved living in the country. I was a tomboy, and there were trees to climb, sand to play and dig in, and under the house in a pile of bricks lived a large, fascinating blue-black indigo snake.

The old house stood on a well drained sand hill. The yard was heaven to all kinds of snakes. The first year we lived there we killed 13 ground rattlers and several diamondback rattlers, as well as a coral snake in the yard. Black snakes, coach-whips, spread adders, and corn snakes were among the nonpoisonous varieties which were also abundant.

Marvin Wilson, unknown boy, and Neal Eichholz holding dead rattlesnake in front of the old house. About 1946.

Other discoveries in our new yard included two kumquat trees hidden at first by the large oak in front of the house. Behind the house were orange trees - sweet oranges we could eat and sour oranges for orangeade and pies. Beside an old barn by the outhouse were pear and persimmon trees. To the right of the house in an old field were several pecan trees.

And that unsafe, forbidden barn was one of my favorite places. It, too, was gray and sagging, with cracks between the boards, but it held a collection of the most interesting things, like old mule collars, plows, bridles, barrels, buckets, and other things which I didn't recognize. Exciting, interesting initials, dates, and names such as Miles Stratton were carved into the weathered walls.

A ladder near the door led to the loft, the floor of which was nearly gone. This part of the barn was particularly forbidden. But from up there I could survey my kingdom. I could examine treasures I hadn't known existed. I could daydream and make believe. And above all, I felt so deliciously wicked in this forbidden, unsafe place.

The old barn past the grapevine is shown from the back of the house where the hand pump was.

Over the years the barn collapsed. A new well with a hand pump replaced the enclosed hole in the ground with a roof and a bucket on a rope when the latter dried up (it was nice not to have to worry about pulling the bucket up with a snake in it.) Forest fire took the persimmon and pear trees, and a freeze killed all the citrus trees. And finally, in 1953, electricity came to our neck of the woods.

We had lived in the old house for 12 years when I got sick with rheumatic fever. While I was in the hospital, Mama had a Jim Walter frame house started. She was determined not to bring me home to the old, damp, un-insulated place. I was released from the hospital early, and came home about a week before the new house was ready to live in, and that was the last week we spent in "Daddy's Bargain."

Once There Was a Place Called Sampson

Latrell, Rosetta, & Terrene Pappy, Sampson, abt. 1946.

Sadly, the old house is gone now. It had become too unsafe, and Mama and Daddy were afraid a hurricane would blow it over. However, it still stood next to the new one when I got married a year later. My husband and I lived in Ohio where he was stationed in the Air Force. The first time we came home, the old house was gone, and I cried as hard as I had when I first saw it. The house I hated had become the home I hadn't known I loved.

Daddy's Bargain *was first published in* North Florida Living, *pages 48/49, August, 1995, North Florida Publishing Co., Inc., 6000 NW 17th Place, Gainesville, Florida, 32605, John Paul Jones, Jr., President and Publisher.* I have made a couple of corrections since it's first publication.

Mullet on the Beach!

An evening breeze blew over Grandpa's porch. Sunday supper was over. Men, children and several dogs lounged on the porch swing, floor, and steps. From the kitchen the sound of women's voices, the tinkle of glass, and the jingle of silverware drifted to us.

This was Palm Valley, Florida, in 1946. The road which wound through the valley and past Grandpa's house was brick. The occasional vehicle, traveling at much slower speeds than today, could be heard for minutes before coming around the bend and into sight of Grandpa's porch. Indeed, the road was so sparsely traveled that any traffic was enough to arouse those of us who had drifted off into the lethargic sleep of people who are too well fed.

Even the sounds from the kitchen halted as a Model T Ford came into view, arms waving from the windows as the car passed on its way to take the news to others. "Mullet on the beach! Mullet on the beach!" called the driver and his passenger.

Suddenly everyone was wide awake. The women's voices had an excited pitch as they wound up their job in the kitchen. The men headed for outbuildings, some for wash tubs, and others for croaker sacks and cast nets. We kids headed for the kitchen, all talking at once, "Mama, can we go, too? Can we get wet? Can we pick up fish?"

In 1946, mullet on the beach was a family affair. To some of us, it still is. Everyone loaded up into several vehicles, and we drove the few miles to Mickler's Landing. Arriving just at dusk, the men took their nets from the cars. Women and children carried the tubs and sacks to the water's edge.

The tide was out and just starting to turn. Rivulets began to trickle into sloughs as the men began to cast their nets. Their trained eyes could see fish run beneath the surface. The schooling fish were so thick they bumped into legs and were occasionally stepped on.

As the nets settled on the fish, leads around the edge anchored on the bottom, trapping the mullet. The tops of the nets bounced up as mullet jumped in their attempts to escape. A sizzling, frying sound signaled nets full of frantic fish to us on the shore, as the men began to pull and carry their loads to us. Once on shore, the men emptied the nets onto the beach, while women and children picked up the mullet and put them into the burlap bags.

Picking up flopping mullet is an art in itself. Grabbing a slippery mullet in the middle or by its tail is futile. You can pick the same one up a dozen times and drop him just as many times, as the rest flop their way back to the approaching surf. As small children, we learned to "grab them by the noses." Getting a grip on the head is the only way to pick up a mullet, and you don't get finned that way, either.

I can feel the wet sand on my face and in my hair, feel the grit between my teeth, the slime from the fish on my hands, and smell the odor of fish and salt water, as I remember that night and others like it. When psychologists speak of spending quality time with children, these simple joys are the times from my childhood that come to mind.

The men followed the schooling fish along the edge of the water. They walked with knees bent like living springs ready to uncoil in a split second. Part of the net was thrown over a shoulder, part in each hand, and part between the teeth. The hand line was wrapped around the wrist.

As we followed the men along the water's edge, we marveled each time a net was cast and opened as perfectly round as a silver dollar. Each time the nets were emptied, we put the fish in the croaker sacks and then emptied the croaker sacks into the wash tubs when they got too heavy to carry. When the tubs were filled, there was enough water in the sloughs for us kids to have a short "swim" before leaving the beach.

Back at Grandpa's, the youngest of us were rinsed in the shower and put to bed, but everyone else cleaned fish into the wee hours of the morning. Grandpa had an electric generator and a refrigerator, marvelous inventions that at that time had not made their way to our community of Sampson, some 15 miles away.

Some of the fish were put in the refrigerator. Some fish were split open to lay flat with the scales left on. These were put in grandpa's smokehouse and the smoking process begun right away. Some were prepared to fry the next day. Some would be boiled with onions and datil peppers to be eaten on rice. But most were salted down in large crocks to be kept for later use. Nothing was wasted, because Grandpa's pigs feasted on the heads and insides.

1946. That was more than 50 years ago. Palm Valley Road, now called 210 East, is no longer brick, and a steady stream of cars now travels it. Grandpa's house no longer stands. Grandpa and Daddy have both gone to their eternal rewards.

You can't drive on the beach at Mickler's Landing anymore (pronounce that Mike-ler's Landing, please), and you wouldn't dare leave your car in a parking lot at night for fear of having it broken into.

Besides, it's unlikely you could walk onto the beach and find mullet near enough to one of the scarce parking lots to be able to carry all your gear down and bring it back with fish. Also, mullet travel along the beach and must be followed, or better yet, be gotten ahead of by fishermen.

However, we still fish for mullet on St. Johns County beaches, at least this year. In fact, St. Johns may be the only county in Florida that still allows any driving on the beach. That could change any time, though. The issue frequently comes before the county commission, as special interest groups and environmentalists attempt to ban vehicles from the beach. In fact, we may now be facing our biggest threat ever to driving on the beach.

We use a four wheel drive vehicle, as wind and water constantly change the beach. At some times and some places we can only drive at low tide. A powerful spotlight which plugs into the cigarette lighter is necessary to spot the fish at night. We drive slowly along the beach as close to the water as possible, shining the light on the water. When the light finds mullet, some will jump up over the surface.

My husband, Yulee, and whichever of our sons who might be with us, cast their nets in the same way Grandpa and Daddy did. The grand kids and wives pick up the mullet the same way I did as a child, but we now use a five gallon plastic bucket instead of a croaker sack, and we transfer them to a cooler of ice instead of a washtub.

Yulee Mickler casting over mullet, Vilano Beach, St. Augustine, July 1982; photo by author.

Not only have we continued a tradition begun by our Minorcan ancestors who came to Florida in 1768, we have passed it down to our children and grandchildren. It is good, clean, wholesome, family fun; it puts nutritious, fresh fish on the table; and it brings memories, a smile, and happiness to those friends and relatives with whom we share.

Those of us who have lived here for generations are probably more scarce than sea turtles the regulations profess to protect. We have already seen so many of our traditions and so much of our culture become endangered and disappear forever. Now uncontrolled growth in our beach communities and a steady migration of people into Florida has us hard pressed to find access to OUR beaches. Some say the days when driving on the beach anywhere will be allowed are numbered. With a sinking heart, I am forced to admit they could be right.

Sea turtle laying eggs, Vilano Beach, 1986; photo by author.

Let the public have what little bit of beach there is left between the dunes/dwellings and the water, and don't put further restrictions on when or where we can drive on OUR beach. Accesses are so few and far between that without vehicular traffic on the beach, miles more of it would become private property, completely lost to public use. In fact, the only time it would be public property is when there was a need for more tax dollars to pay for re-nourishment to prevent those private structures and properties from being destroyed by wind and waves.

Although mullet may not be as plentiful as they were fifty years ago, they aren't in short supply. Many newcomers even turn their noses up at this delicious fish. However, for those of us to whom mullet fishing is a tradition, a sport, a family outing, and an important source of fish in our diets, I hope and pray that St. Johns County will leave those of us who have called Florida home for generations, something of our heritage, at least when there's "mullet on the beach!"

Bucket of mullet; photo by author.

P.S.

Due to some who are privileged enough to own expensive beach homes, the proliferation of beach condos [whose inhabitants want private beaches], and the environmental claims of protection of sea turtles and their nests, no lights, including vehicle lights, are allowed on any of our beaches during half of the year which includes spring and summer. No night driving, when mullet fishing is best, is allowed on our beaches at all. The claim is that the lights from vehicular traffic and beach houses causes the baby turtles to get confused and go in the wrong direction, and that the cars crush the turtle nests. Another heritage has been stripped from area natives by transplants and overreaching bureaucrats.)

Mullet on the Beach *was first published in* The Creekline, *pages 1, 14-15, October, 2002, RT Publishing, Inc., One San Jose Place, Suite 21, Jacksonville, FL 32257, Publisher Rebecca Taus. ("Grandpa was William Mickler of Palm Valley, and" Daddy" was Terrell Pappy of Sampson.)*

Gopher Stew

Recent comers and guests in Florida immediately think of a furry rodent when locals mention gopher stew. The local gopher is not related at all to the rat family, however. It is a tortoise whose scientific name is gopherus polyphemus. The only thing it has in common with the rodent gopher besides its name is the fact that it lives in a hole in the ground.

Photo by author.

When the Minorcans came to Florida in the 1760s, gophers were plentiful, and the starving colonists soon discovered them. Prime gopher habitat was also abundant. Much of Florida was undeveloped sand hill country which the gophers thrived in. Since then, the sand hills have become favored by developers, and Florida's timber industry has taken its toll on the gopher's habitat, too. While the gopher-eating population has increased, the gopher population has declined.

Because of declining populations, the gopher is now protected. The Florida Game and Fresh Water Fish Commission regulations allow the taking of gophers only from July 1 to January 1. It is illegal to shoot, snare, or use bucket traps to take gophers, and a person may possess only two. [NOTE: Since this article was first written, gophers have been placed on the threatened species list, and no taking of them is allowed.]

However, in the mid-1940s, we used to get 50 to 100 gophers on weekend expeditions that several other families and my own took together. These gopher hunting and pulling trips were recreation for everyone involved, and were usually to a place in Clay County known to us as Twelve Oaks. Here we camped, sleeping on quilts spread under the oaks, the starry sky our roof.

During the day while Mama watched us children and took us swimming in the nearby creek the men and the other women located and pulled gophers. The gopher holes were easy to find, because the gophers left yellow mounds of sand at the mouths of their burrows. It was very important not to get near the front of the hole; rattlesnakes often shared the gopher's home, as well as indigo and gopher snakes and other small animals and insects.

Gopher poles, axes, and shovels were the necessary tools for taking the elusive animals. The poles were made of cypress and were about one and a half inches in diameter and 14 feet long. The business end had a steel rod three and a half to four feet long with the end bent about 90 degrees to form a hook. The trick was to get the hook down the hole until the gopher was felt, then to maneuver the hook under the back part of the top shell and turn it so it would hold the gopher while it was pulled from its burrow.

An article in *Florida Wildlife*, January 1979, "The Gopher" by. E. L. Mathews said gophers were ensnared in bedsprings on the ends of limber rods and pulled from their holes. I never knew of anyone to use a coiled bed spring to entangle a gopher, as gopher holes frequently twist and turn and are often obstructed by roots. However, the frame of the bedsprings is used as mentioned earlier, and this is approximately a 3/8 inch rod, much sturdier than the spring itself.

Besides the gopher pole, the shovel was used to dig out the hole if it made a sharp turn, or to get to a root that interfered with pulling the gopher out. The axe was used to cut small trees at the mouth of the hole that prevented maneuvering the pole, and to chop away roots after they were exposed with the shovel.

After the gophers were pulled, they were cleaned at the creek, and all of us were involved. The gophers were put in the shallow water at the edge. We younger kids would watch them so they didn't escape. The reason for submerging them was to remove the sand and to get the shy creatures to take their heads out of their shells so they could be decapitated. The gopher was picked up by its head so the animal wouldn't be able to pull it back in.

Next, the men would chop down each side of the shell with a hatchet so the shells could be removed. The liver, tripe and eggs (if there were any) were removed by the women, and saved. Then the legs and fleshy parts were severed loose. All the butchering occurred on a makeshift table - the little wooden bridge over the creek, and the creek water was used to wash the meat.

More creek water was boiled over a campfire, and the parts with skin were scalded. The outer skin was scraped and peeled off. The ends of the feet containing the toenails were trimmed off, and the gopher was ready to be cooked, usually over an open fire in a huge iron pot.

Gopher stew is a Minorcan gourmet's delight, and we still eat it when we can get it. We pull the gophers the same way, but weekend trips aren't needed (alas!) to get the two gophers allowed. The gophers are usually cleaned in the back yard, scalded and scraped in the kitchen. The gopher pole we now use is similar, except that now the three and a half to four foot rod with the hook is extended by the addition of a 10 foot piece of aluminum. This assembly is attached to the 10 foot pole or handle. We can no longer be so choosy about the type of wood we use for the handle, either. We use fir or whatever soft wood is available. [Remember, this article was written before it became illegal.]

Leatta & Josephine Pappy in front; Phelza and Eva Wilson in back, preparing gopher meat for cooking at Twelve Oaks, abt. 1946.

However, we are fortunate to have one of the same cooks to cook our gopher stew, and she uses the same recipe. She is my mother, Josephine Pappy, and is known as the master chef of gopher stew by those who have eaten her delicious concoction. She uses an old Minorcan recipe handed down through the generations and modified only by the use of processed tomatoes and flour. Here it is:

Minorcan Gopher Stew

>The meat of 2 medium cleaned and prepared gophers
>2 onions, sliced
>1 (16 ounce) can tomatoes
>½ pound salt pork, diced
>flour
>salt, black pepper, and datil pepper to taste

Fry bacon in a 6 quart pot, heavy and preferably cast iron. Remove the bacon and all but about 1 tablespoon of bacon drippings from the pan and reserve for later use.

Brown the pieces of gopher with skin in the tablespoon of drippings. Next, add the fleshy pieces of gopher and the tripe. Cook down until the liquid comes out of it.

Brown chopped onions in a frying pan with one tablespoon of the bacon drippings. Add the pieces of bacon and the tomatoes with the juice. Chop tomatoes into small pieces with a spoon, and cook down slowly on lowest heat until all the liquid is gone. Stir frequently to prevent sticking.

After the tomatoes are cooked down, add to the gopher pot. Add enough water to make the amount of gravy you want. Put the livers in the pot. Add salt and pepper.

Brown the flour in the remaining drippings. Reserve. Boil gopher stew until the meat is tender (Medium gophers usually take 2-3 hours to cook, while large gophers, which are usually tough, can take as long as 6-7 hours.) Next, add browned flour to thicken. Then add chopped datil peppers to taste. Return to boil, add eggs and turn the stove off.

This delicious Minorcan dish is eaten over rice.

In the words of an old gopher eater, "Tastes so good it makes your tongue slap your jaw teeth out."

P.S.

Josephine Pappy, my mother, died in 2005; May God have mercy on her soul.

Gophers are now on the endangered species list, and are protected by the federal government. It is against the law to take or possess ANY. What is particularly galling is the fact that for a price, developers can plow them under or pave them over, but when a head of the Environmental Department of the City of Jacksonville was asked a few years ago if someone could remove gophers to eat that were going to be destroyed by developers, the answer was, "Absolutely not!" It seems hypocritical to me to allow an endangered species to be destroyed for a price, and yet, illegal for that which is destined for destruction to be eaten, thus preventing waste of a good food source. But such is the wisdom of our governing officials and environmental agencies.

Gopher Stew *was first published in* North Florida Living, *pages 68, 76/77, January 1986, The North Florida Publishing Co., Inc., 6000 NW 17th Place, Gainesville, Fla., 32605, John Paul Jones, Jr., President* **&** *Publisher.* The P.S. was added for this book.

Monsignor Dawson Remembers St. Joseph's

St. Joseph's Rectory & Church before the road was paved in about 1928. Father Dawson lived in this rectory as did following pastors until recently. Photo in the possession of the author.

In February of 1957, Father Joseph Dawson became pastor of St. Joseph's Catholic Church in Loretto. During a visit to Monsignor Dawson at his home in Georgia recently, we discussed the parish during the time he was pastor.

According to Monsignor Dawson, there was no San Jose Parish at the time; Assumption was the nearest parish, and no one was sure where the boundary was. That made it impossible to be sure how many parishioners there were, but he said about 150 families regularly attended Mass at St. Joseph's.

The convent was still there, but it burned while he was pastor. The present school was started while the previous pastor, Father Burns, was here. The school had eight grades. Monsignor Dawson remembers the church had a mortgage and a modest income. Everyone helped, however, and there were two bazaars to help raise money for the two mortgage payments.

He recalled a flood in the school building. The architect had put the main hot water pipes under the slab without expansion joints. When he called the architect, he was told the building was no longer under warranty. The building was also infested with termites, and that warranty had also lapsed. He called Paul Danese, plumber by trade, and always there when called upon to help the church. Paul dug up the old floor and repaired it all.

Of St. Joseph's, Monsignor said, "It was the most cohesive parish I have ever been in. It was so small, but everyone helped. Each person would do what he knew how to do. There was always somebody to do what ever was needed. Everyone knew everyone else, and if someone couldn't do something, he knew someone who could. The parish would never have made it without the generosity of its members."

He was hesitant to mention particular people, because he didn't want to leave anyone out, but he said he called most on those who lived nearest the church. He said, "Josephine Danese Carter lived across the road from the church. She played the organ for Mass, weddings, and funerals, all for the love of God. Of course, all the women helped. They took care of all the altar linens, washed and ironed them, and did whatever else they could. Emmanuel Danese helped with real estate matters. If anything went wrong, I would call Cecil Sparkman. He was always helping out. Maurice Danese was an electrician. He took care of all the fluorescent lights for the school for free. It took an electrician to change the ballasts in them. Paul and Louis Danese Sr. took care of the plumbing. Oscar Lott painted the signs.

"One day I came back from the chancery – there was a sand floor in the garage – I got out of the car and was immediately covered with fleas. A mangy dog had died in the garage. Oscar Lott was the closest parishioner, so I called him and he took care of the fleas."

He remembered Gerald Lourcey cutting down a huge camphor tree for the parish and recalled he was in the tree cutting business. He had heard that Gerald also carried a previous pastor, Father Rockett, to Palm Valley to hold Mass before there was a church nearer there.

During the Viet Nam War, Archbishop Hurley asked for volunteers to serve the men in the military. Father Dawson volunteered. He took a leave of absence from St. Joseph. During the three years he was gone, Father Corde "took excellent care of the parish." He returned to St. Joseph's in January of 1969. He said, "What really supported the church was volunteer assistance from all the qualified people in the church. It formed a bond of unity among the people. They all gave their time and talent to make up for lack of money. I tried to be careful, to live frugally within the means available.

When asked what his best memories of St. Joseph's were, he said, "I've already given you the answer to that. What I remember most about St. Joseph's is how cooperative the people were. They made dedicated sacrifices of their time and convenience to take care of the needs of the parish. They certainly did that before I came and after I left."

MONSIGNOR JOSEPH L. DAWSON

In a follow-up with Monsignor Dawson, his final comment to me was, "May God bless all the members of the parish."

Monsignor Joseph Dawson, born December 29, 1936, died January 4, 2002, of cancer of the spine.

Monsignor Dawson Remembers St. Joseph's *was first published in* St. Joseph's Reflections, *date unknown.*

St. Joseph's Catholic Church is in Loretto near Mandarin, Duval County, Florida. From the small parish described in this article, it has grown to probably the largest parish in the state with about 5,000 families registered.

Sinister Insects: First Aid Afield

Florida with its climate, beauty and opportunities for outdoor adventures is host to people of all ages, incomes, and interests. Just as everyone can enjoy Florida's outdoors, all need to be aware of the potential for injury, of prevention methods, and how to give first aid afield.

Prevention begins with keeping anti-tetanus immunizations up to date. Just about any injury from bee stings to compound fractures can introduce the tetanus germ into your body.

Basic first aid techniques, including artificial respiration and cardiopulmonary resuscitation (CPR) are best learned by taking courses such as those taught by the American Red Cross before your outdoor adventure. Should you find yourself alone with someone who needs one or more of these techniques for survival, you may not have time to look them up in your first aid manual.

Insect & Spider Bites

Insects and arachnids (spiders and their kin) can inflict bites that cause annoying itches, pain, diseases, and even death. A good insect repellent with diethyl-metatoluamide (DEET) is effective in repelling many offending creatures.

After a bite or sting, steps must be taken at once to control the venom and symptoms, which may be severe right away or several hours later, especially if there are multiple bites or stings or venom allergy. Asthmatics, those who suffer from hay fever and/or other allergies, are more likely to be allergic to venom, according to Maynard Cox, snake expert and poison bite specialist.

Anaphalaxtic shock symptoms include swelling to the body other than at the site of the bite or sting; throat constriction; wheezing; rapid, shallow breath; nausea; vomiting and/or clammy skin. Treat for shock. If the victim has an anaphalaxtic sting kit, use it. Get the victim to a hospital immediately.

Ticks

Ticks are abundant in Florida, particularly in warm months. Some carry diseases in their saliva that can be transferred to your bloodstream. Maynard Cox recommends, "When a tick bites, you should remove it carefully by: (1) wiping the tick with an alcohol swab, grasping the tick as close to the head as possible, and pulling with a slow, steady tension until the tick lets go. Coat the tick with clear fingernail polish. Save it in an envelope or plastic bag with the date of the bite written on it; or (2) on parts of the body where there is little hair, clear nail polish can be painted on the attached tick.

"Ticks breathe through openings on each side of the hindquarters of their bodies. The nail polish suffocates the tick as it dries, causing the tick to back out into the hardening polish. When completely dry, the nail polish seals the tick into a neat, plastic package which you should keep as above for identification by a bite specialist should any symptoms occur. Don't use colored polish, as this makes identification impossible."

Tick bites should be washed with warm, soapy water and treated with a broad spectrum antibiotic ointment such as Bacitracin or Neosporin.

"Tick bites are usually raised and pink, but should the head and body parts remain in the bite site, infection may occur which requires surgical removal of tick remains," says Cox.

All ticks can transmit fever and paralysis (tick bite fever). Three are capable of transmitting Rocky Mountain Spotted Fever (RMSF). Two are known to transmit Lyme disease.

Because tick saliva carries the disease-bearing organisms and also has a substance that keeps blood from clotting, the tick must normally stay attached for at least several hours to transmit the disease. Grabbing the tick by the body when removing it can force its body contents into the bite, thus aiding infection.

Careful search of your and your children's bodies frequently when in tick infested areas, and proper removal of ticks will help prevent infection. Wash hands that touch ticks with soap and water, as well as the bite area.

Rocky Mountain Spotted Fever carriers are the lone star tick, wood tick, and eastern dog tick (see drawing). Should symptoms occur and the tick is identified as a RMSF carrier, blood tests will determine whether the victim has the disease. If the tick bite isn't mentioned, it may be misdiagnosed, as it resembles many other diseases. Symptoms appear in 3 to 18 days and may include fever, watery eyes and a rash that erupts into open sores.

Any unexplained muscular weakness, especially in a child, calls for a careful search for ticks, especially in hairy body areas. Paralysis resulting from tick fever can result in death. Removal of the tick usually causes the symptoms to stop quickly. Symptoms usually occur in 3 - 18 days, but may occur from 10 hours to 24 days.

The deer tick nymph, about the size of the dot on an "i" before bloating on a blood meal, is the chief carrier of Lyme disease. After bloating, Cox says it resembles a blood blister with legs. The lone star tick, which has reached Florida, can also transmit Lyme disease.

Lyme disease is caused by a bacteria found in some deer, white-footed mice, quail and other warm-blooded animals, including dogs and cats. The tick gets the bacteria from biting infected animals and may be passed from adult tick to larvae. The blood of infected animals can also transmit the disease, a fact that should be noted by hunters. Only infected dogs and humans get sick from it.

Should a circular red rash with a clear center develop where a tick bit, tell your doctor and ask for a blood test for Lyme disease. Early treatment with tetracycline or penicillin can prevent the serious symptoms that can mimic malaria, arthritis, multiple sclerosis, Lou Gehrig's disease, and Alzheimers. It can damage joints, lungs, spleen, kidneys, liver, eyes, heart, brain, and nervous system.

Deer ticks are prevalent here in the grass and brush all year. "The best weapon against ticks is fire; controlled burning by timber managers is of great assistance in tick control," says Cox.

"Camphho-Phenique applied to the cuffs of long pants and sleeves and around collars destroys the tick's nerve endings and prevents attachment to the skin. Use carefully; it can irritate your skin.

"Avon's Skin-So-Soft used full strength on bare skin, applied frequently or applied directly to clothing where it lasts longer, sometimes works for ticks as well as for other pests.

"Use of an insect repellent with DEET on clothes and shoes is effective in repelling ticks. Effective repellents; careful search, removal, preservation, and bite information; use of soap and water and an antibiotic ointment may prevent a tick from making you or your child sick," says Cox.

Poisonous Spiders

Florida is also home to the poisonous brown, red, and the more common black widow and brown recluse spiders.

The widow often makes its web in outbuildings or protected spots outdoors, across toilet seats, waste cans, branches and shrubs. During the day the widow usually remains out of sight, according to Cox.

Its bite usually causes a sharp pain like a needle prick and usually contains three puncture holes in a raised, white spot with a red edge, which lasts up to four hours; while in minutes to several hours later local muscular cramps begin. The venom causes motor paralysis and destruction of nerve endings. The pain worsens, spreading to the abdomen; weakness and shaking develop; breathing is affected. The symptoms may be confused with appendicitis. Symptoms worsen for several hours to a day, become less severe in two to three days. Weakness, tingling, nervousness, and muscle spasms may come and go for months.

"*Do not cut, suction or tourniquet* a spider or any other bite. Treatment at the bite site is of no value. Hospitalize the victim for widow spider antivenin, the only known neutralizer of widow spider venom. Early use brings prompt relief," says Cox.

The brown recluse spider, also called the brown house spider, brown spider, or fiddleback spider (it has a dark, fiddle-shaped area on its back), varies in color from gray-brown to deep red-brown, with a large, fuzzy abdomen. It lives in sheltered outdoor areas, under rocks and loose bark but dry, littered, insect-infested buildings attract them also. They often hide in clothing left hanging in outbuildings.

Usually the bite causes intense pain, but sometimes the victim doesn't know he's been bitten and won't feel discomfort for an hour or so. A small white blister appears where the fangs punctured the skin. The site will enlarge, turn red and harden in one to eight hours. Eventually the area will peel away. The center will sink, become bluish-black ringed by a red, raised area with a white outer edge. It is hot to the touch and resembles a mini volcano. An ulcerating sore develops. Victims have had chills, rash, fever, bloody urine, weakness, jaundice and/or convulsions. Cox says healing is slow and improvement may not become evident for two to six weeks. Shock may occur. Medical attention is essential.

Caterpillars

Many caterpillar and moth larvae sting and cause rashes. To most people the symptoms aren't dangerous unless the victim is severely allergic. However, there are four poisonous caterpillars: the puss and saddleback caterpillars and the IO and hag moth larvae. They have mucoid sacs at the bases of their stinging hairs with hollow spines connected to poison glands. The sting effect ranges from an initial itching, sharp stinging sensation to a pain like that of a red-hot cigarette held to your skin, and is called "mock envenomation syndrome," according to Cox. Considerable numbness is followed by a throbbing ache involving the entire bitten limb. Sometimes nausea, vomiting, severe swelling and shock occurs, lasting up to 48 hours.

Cox advises that you wash the sting area with lots of warm, soapy water. Next, scrub vigorously with household ammonia and a plastic sponge to get under the skin to the poison. Then scrub with one teaspoon each of baking soda and meat tenderizer to a cup of household ammonia into the sting. Then apply a sting aid such as Tetrocaine. Because the spiny hair is broken off under the skin, this may not be 100 percent effective.

Treat for shock. The victim will need medical attention. All four stings are treated the same. Symptoms can be controlled in one to four hours with proper treatment unless the patient is extremely sensitive to the poison; then it may take several days.

Avoid all hairy caterpillars. If on gets on you, brush it off with something other than your hand. Don't crush it. Again, long sleeves and long pants protect most of the body.

Stinging Insects

Bees, wasps, fire ants, yellow jackets and hornets can cause death in less than an hour to those who are allergic to their toxins. Anyone who has ever had even a slight reaction to any of these insects should carry an anaphylactic bite kit (available by prescription), know how to use it, and teach their companions how to use it also. Stings on veins and arteries can be serious. Honeybees leave their stingers in the wound. Remove by scraping it off, so as not to force more venom into the wound. A paste of baking soda or household ammonia will lessen the pain.

Cox's advice: avoid the insects by avoiding flowering plants; don't go barefoot; keep sweet items covered; stand still if one is near; if it lights on you, brush, don't slap it off; don't wear brightly colored, especially flower printed, clothing or perfumed concoctions.

The velvet ant is really a wingless wasp ½ to one inch long. It stings only when handled or trapped, as in clothing, or stepped on barefoot.

Wheel bugs bite when accidentally contacted by people. Their salivary fluid causes an immediate pain which lasts three to six hours. The southern centipede inflicts a painful bite which causes a two puncture wound with local inflammation, swelling, and soreness. The burning, aching pain usually lasts about five hours. Wash well with soap and water. Apply a wet Epsom Salt poultice. The severe pain will require medical attention.

Scorpion

The Florida scorpion causes a strong local inflammation, but its sting is not serious unless there is hypersensitivity. Its stinger is at the end of its tail. Campers should check clothing and shoes before getting dressed as scorpions may hide in them. Wash stings with soap and water, and apply a sting aid.

Water Bug

The water bug or giant electric light bug grows to more than two inches long. It lives in water, but is attracted to strong light at night. It has a strong beak which causes a painful, burning sensation when it bites. The area swells, becomes red. Pain continues for some time. The baking soda, tenderizer and ammonia mixture alleviates the pain.

Blister Beetle

Blister beetles contain a toxin in body fluids that causes blisters. Crushing one on the skin causes a sharp pain like a splash of hot oil. A blister forms later. A wet Epson Salt poultice will ease the pain.

Red Bugs

Red bugs (chiggers) are tiny tick-like creature that burrow into the skin and cause intense itching. Scratching can cause infection. First aid for all itching bites should alleviate itching and prevent infection. Products such as Campho-Phenique, Chigger rid, After Bite, Foille, and Sting Kill are effective. If not available, the ammonia mixture will help, or whichever of the three ingredients you have, advises Cox.

Spanish moss, the long, gray, beard-like growth on many Florida trees, is a favorite haunt of red bugs. Avoid handling Spanish moss.

Sitting directly on the ground is an invitation for redbugs to crawl on your body. When they come to elastic or a tight waistband, etc., they dig in. The same things that repel ticks will repel red bugs.

Mosquitoes

The use of insect repellents with DEET are effective in preventing mosquitoes (which carry encephalitis), yellow, horse, deer, black, dog, and other flies from biting. Avon's Skin-So-Soft is also effective, however its sweet smell may attract bees, etc. Treating the bites with an after-bite preparation alleviates itching. These insects are usually more of a nuisance than a danger.

No matter what you do for relaxation, you run some risk of injury, so don't let this article scare you into stagnation in front of your TV. Learn proper first aid, keep tetanus shots up to date, and educate yourself and your family about the dangers, precautions, and the actions to take in the event an accident occurs. Chances are in your favor nothing will. If it should, you will be able to prevent an unpleasant incident from becoming a tragedy.

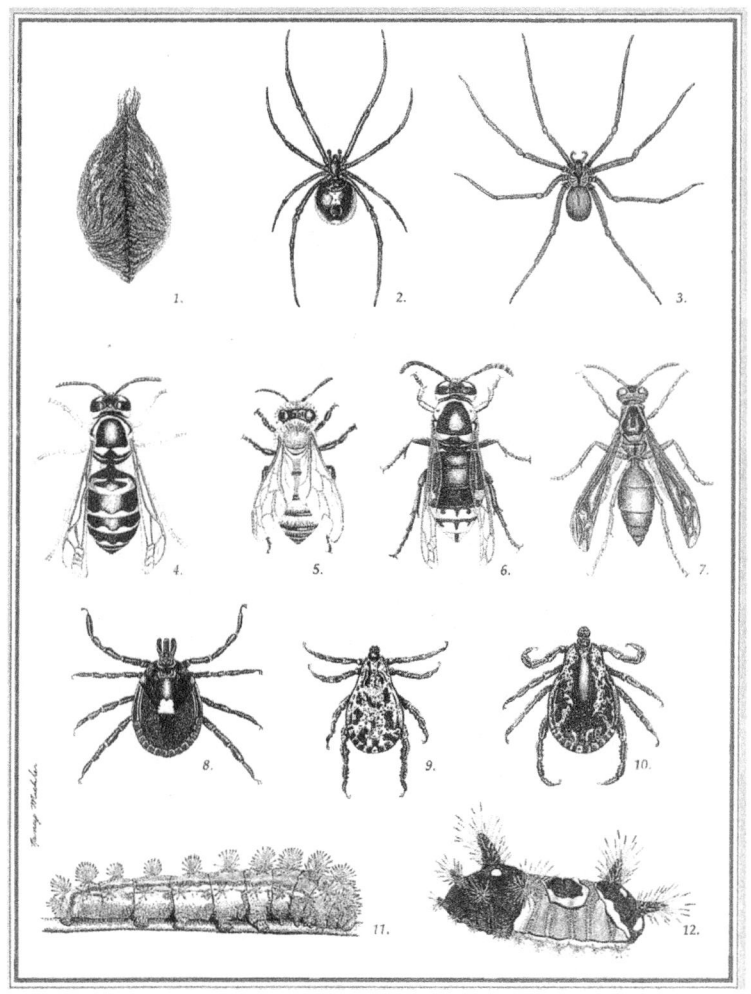

1. Puss caterpillar; 2. Black widow spider, ventral view; 3. Brown recluse spider; 4. yellow jacket; 5. Honey bee; 6. Hornet; 7. Wasp; 8. Lone star tick; 9. Eastern dog tick; 10. Wood tick; 11. IO moth larva; 12. Saddleback caterpillar. Illustrated by Nancy Mickler.

Sinister Insects: First Aid Afield *was first published in* Florida Woods and Waters, *May/June 1990 Issue, pages 24,32-33; Grace Hawkins, T.T. Publications, Inc., 346 N. Freeman St., Longwood, Florida 32750. The illustration is pen and ink, originally in color, by Nancy Mickler, the author's daughter, and used with her permission.*

Poisonous Mouth of the River

Those who frequent the great Florida outdoors should be aware of a unique hazard. The weather is often warm, the ground frequently wet, and a sinister species often crawls on the forest floor or lies on the branches of trees over water where people walk, fish, swim, and boat.

One afternoon during spring gobbler season I had a close encounter with this dangerous creature, as my husband and I were attempting to roost turkeys. At the edge of the swamp, my spouse pointed and said, "Sit under that big oak, and I'll go down the swamp a couple of hundred yards."

As I approached the oak, I noticed a round, dark object. Upon cautiously creeping to within 10 feet, I realized it was a coiled cottonmouth moccasin. Its dark body made a circle about 14 inches in diameter. The snake opened its mouth in a silent threat, revealing a white interior. A few feet from this snake lay another of the coiled vipers.

This is not an isolated occurrence. Those who look carefully and know what they are looking for, frequently see moccasins in the Florida woods. And those who do not see them encounter them just as often. Needless to say, this hunter found another place to listen for the sounds of turkeys flying into their roosting trees.

This isn't to scare outdoor lovers, or to advocate the elimination of cottonmouth moccasins. The cottonmouth, like other snakes, has its place in the ecological scheme. It helps to control the rodent population, which can be so harmful and destructive to crops and carries so many diseases. Rather, it is to inform people who engage in outdoor activities of the existence of the creature, its habits and danger, how to recognize and avoid it, and what to do if bitten by one of the venomous vipers.

The cottonmouth lives along the banks of rivers, streams, lakes, man-made pits and ditches, and in swamps and marshes throughout the state. But those who think that moccasins are found only near water had better think again. Experts says moccasins often leave the wet areas when about 2 ½ feet in length to enter the open piney woods. Here they feed on small mammals.

Daniel McCook is a herpetologist at the St. Augustine Alligator Farm. He begins his speech and demonstration on reptiles by pulling a cottonmouth moccasin from a metal trunk to the gasps and groans of his audience. Someone can invariably be heard to say, "That guy's crazy!" as McCook goes on with his show. He explains that the word moccasin is an Indian word that means "mouth of the River."

This "mouth of the river," the cottonmouth moccasin, belongs to the Crotalidae, or pit viper family. Its scientific name is Agkistrodon piscivorus. Other pit vipers in Florida are diamondback and canebrake rattlesnakes and pygmy rattlers. They all have a lorel pit between they eye and nostril. "This pit gives them the ability to sense small warm-blooded animals up to 14 feet away and find them in total darkness," says Maynard H. Cox, founder and director of the World Wide Poison Bite Information Center in Orange Park, Florida. Their eyes have elliptical pupils, and the heads are arrow-shaped and wider than the neck.

McCook cautions that you shouldn't use the above criteria to attempt to identify a snake in the wild, though. "You'd have to be about three inches away to see his elliptical pupils, and nobody wants to get that close to a moccasin." McCook, who describes himself as a professional-amateur herpetologist, has worked with snakes for more than twenty years. He says, "The best way to tell a moccasin from a nonpoisonous snake is by a chocolate band, or stripe, that runs through the eye and back to his jaw. This band can be seen from five to eight feet away."

Cottonmouths frequently grow to more than five feet in length, but average about three feet. They are green-brown to black and sometimes have dark cross-bands on their bodies. The younger snakes are more brightly colored, with yellow or copper markings. (Experts say those who believe they have seen a copperhead in

Florida have most likely seen a young cottonmouth, as the coloring and markings is sometimes nearly identical.)

Moccasins have thick bodies and tails that taper abruptly. Maynard Cox says, "There are no long whip-like tail poisonous snakes in the whole USA." There are yellowish spots on the belly and throat of the moccasin, and the inside of the mouth is white, hence the name cottonmouth.

Coiled cottonmouth moccasin. Photo by author.

Cottonmouth moccasins don't have to be coiled to strike, and they can and do strike under water. However, a disturbed moccasin usually coils and opens its mouth. Since it is so well camouflaged, the white interior of its mouth is an easily seen warning to its would-be victims. Cox says that cottonmouth moccasins hold their heads at a 45 degree angle, whether crawling, swimming, lying straight, or coiled.

Contrary to the beliefs of some, all snakes lay eggs except a garter snake in Nova Scotia, which bears its young live. However, Cox adds, they all have the ability to bear their young live under bad weather conditions.

The cottonmouth usually lays five to twelve eggs which hatch striking. According to Cox, they are as poisonous the minute they hatch as the minute they die.

Several years ago a game warden for the state related this story: A young boy was fishing with a cane pole. Another game warden asked the boy if he was having any luck. The boy answered no, but said his "worms" were biting him. Upon inspection, the game warden determined the boy's "worms" were actually baby moccasins, and the boy's hands had indeed been bitten several times. The boy died in spite of medical treatment.

The bite of the cottonmouth is extremely painful and can be fatal to human beings. However, Cox maintains that a victim who dies within the first 30 minutes after snakebite dies not from the bite, but from shock. Cox is an authority on the treatment of snakebite. He has studied snakes for 48 years and has authored a book, *Protocol for Emergency Room Procedures and Hospital Management of Snakebite* for use by doctors in treating snakebite victims. He says pain and/or panic cause shock. Pit vipers' salivary proteins cause an acute inflammatory state of immunoglobulin which causes a pain "like burning fire." Add to that the terror most people feel at the mere thought of snake bite, and shock is inevitable.

Cox says those who die in the first 30 minutes have usually been bitten on one of the four main body pipelines - blood vein, lymphatic vein, nerve trunk, or artery, AND the snake has injected venom. (He maintains that in 40% of cases, the snake does not inject venom.) These areas are more sensitive to pain. Cox is one of the very few people to survive direct intravenous injection of snake venom. Although he has been bitten 136 times, only twice were the bites on a main pipeline. In 1978 he was bitten on the right ring finger by a baby diamondback less than 18" long, and last year on the left middle finger by a five foot long diamondback. Incidentally, about 10 of his snake bites were from cottonmouth moccasins.

In 1972, five year old Donna Danese of Sampson, Florida, stepped off the front porch of her rural Florida home onto the waiting fangs of a 2 ½ to 3 foot cottonmouth. She screamed in pain and terror, and didn't quit until after she lost consciousness in the hospital emergency room.

Donna's mother ran to her screaming daughter to see the coiled moccasin, mouth still open and threatening a few feet from the child. Her foot was already swelling and turning dark. Mrs. Danese scooped the child up and ran to the phone to call her father, the late Euzeal Pappy, to take them to the hospital. Pappy, a Florida Wildlife Officer, was her nearest neighbor. He was there in 10 minutes.

When he arrived at the Danese house, the snake still lay coiled by the porch. He killed it and carried it to the hospital in a bucket in the car trunk. The doctor on duty in the emergency room identified the snake as a rattlesnake, even though the game warden, a life-long Florida resident and woodsman, and two Florida road patrolmen who were familiar with snakes, told the doctor it was a moccasin. It was a young snake with bright colors, and the doctor's medical book pictured darker, mature moccasins.

According to snake experts, misidentification of snakes by doctors is about as common as misidentification by other people who encounter snakes. Snakebite is so rare that most doctors never have the occasion to treat it, and rarely know one snake from another.

Donna was tested for antivenin allergy. Although she was determined to be allergic, the doctor decided she would definitely die without it. By then her foot was huge and completely black.

When the antivenin began to trickle into Donna's arm through the intravenous needle, she immediately went into shock and became unconscious. She was packed in ice.

Pappy told his daughter that when a moccasin bites, the rotting process begins immediately, and gangrene sets in. Any rotting flesh would have to be amputated.

According to McCook, doctors fear moccasin bites more because of infection and gangrene that the venom which is not as potent as the rattlesnake's. A bite on the tip of a finger can cause the loss of a limb, not from the venom, but from infection and gangrene.

Swamps, he contends, are germy and infectious places, and when the venom is sucked out by mouth as some snake bite experts recommend, infection can be caused by oral germs.

Cox says the moccasin's mouth has more numerous types of germs than other snakes, and sometimes harbors Clostridium Perfringens which causes gas gangrene.

Further, McCook says the moccasin has ". . . haemotoxic venom, which means it attacks blood cells and body tissue. You can not become immune to the venom. It's like becoming immune to acid, because it tends to eat away at the flesh and does nasty little things to your internal organs."

Toxins in moccasin and other pit viper venom also affect the respiratory, nervous, and muscular systems, as well as the heart. Cox says, "When a pit viper bites, the poison is walled in by itself at the site of the bite. You have up to twelve hours to seek PROPER (emphasis is Cox's) medical care if you survive the first 30 minutes." However, it makes sense to get that treatment as soon as possible to save yourself pain, and possible complications from infections. "After about twelve hours, the poison begins to break down tissue and the main body organs begin to slow down. The kidneys usually go first, then the lungs, and the victim dies of congestive heart failure," Cox continues.

The day after Donna was bitten, a local doctor, who was familiar with Florida snakes, verified that the snake was indeed a moccasin. But he said the treatment for rattlesnake bite and moccasin bite is the same, as is the antivenin.

Fortunately, Donna did recover and was released from the hospital five days later. Even after 14 years she still remembers the excruciating pain and terror the moccasin inflicted. She and other victims describe the symptoms of pit viper bite as immediate swelling and intense, fiery pain at and near the bite, and aching all over. There is also nausea and sweating, as well as feeling cold. The victim sometimes loses consciousness.

Mrs. Danese says Donna's doctors told her Donna lost no flesh due to gangrene because of the first aid she received. She was told the treatment a victim gets on the way to the hospital often determines whether there will be gangrene and how much flesh will be lost. Cutting through fang marks can slice veins, arteries, nerves and muscle tissue, causing more flesh loss and gangrene. Then the doctor has to try to repair that as well as treat snakebite.

McCook says, "Snakebite treatment is a controversial and lengthy subject." Try comparing advice in some of the books on the subject if you doubt him. Some advocate tourniquets, while others oppose them; some say cut and suction, others say absolutely not. Other advice includes washing with hot water and soap, immobilization of the bitten part, lowering the bitten part below heart level, and different combinations or eliminations of the above advice. The one thing all advise is that snake bite victims have professional help immediately.

The most up-to-date treatment for snakebite is Maynard Cox. He has been treating snakebite for about 20 years. After treating more than 500 patients, he has lost neither a snakebite victim nor a limb.

First bitten by a diamondback rattler at the age of six, he decided to learn all he could about snakes. He served in Indochina in the Navy and worked with Dr. Tom Dooley in Southeast Asia where they developed the forerunner to his book. He worked with Dr. Newton C. McCullough in Orlando, Florida, from 1956 to 1966, and in 1969 the two of them got together with the Florida State Board of Health and finished research on the McCullough Theory of Aggressive Serum Therapy for Snake Bites.

"In 1971, I went to college and got a degree in medical laboratory diagnostic technology, which I married with herpetology and found myself in a place no one had ever been before," says Cox. He wrote his book and opened the North Florida Snakebite Treatment Center at Naval Air Station, Jacksonville, Florida, Hospital in 1969, using his book as a guide to treating snakebites. Four years later the center moved to Clay Memorial Hospital in Green Cove Springs, Florida. In August of 1985, he closed the center and reorganized as the World Wide Poison Bite Information Center.

In 1973, the Civil Defense Authority provided funds so that he could be contacted "25 hours a day, eight days a week," Cox likes to say.

As a community service, the Clay County Sheriff's Department agreed to allow their phone to be used to contact Cox via a beeper, which he always wears, so that he is constantly available for consultation when someone is snake bitten, or stung, or bitten by anything that poisons, or causes rabies, or for pesticide poisoning.

He lectures in seven southeastern states to people from kindergartners to doctors.

He stresses that PROPER first aid is necessary to save life and limb. His business card outlines proper first aid:

1. Do not cut and suck.
2. Do not apply ice or tourniquet.
3. Treat for shock:
    "If face is pale, raise the tail.
    If face is red, raise the head."

He and McCook agree that cutting increases the damage. Cox says sucking gets such a small amount of poison out, and then only when done immediately, that it doesn't help. Ice can add frostbite to the problem. Tourniquetting can cause complications such as gangrene and loss of limb. It is unnecessary because the poison can't go anywhere for 12 hours anyway.

Cox advises that you get to a hospital immediately and call or have someone call him at 904-264-6512. He isn't a doctor, but is a special advisor for snakebite treatment, and he knows more about snake bites than most doctors.

He cautions that you should keep calm and remember panic is your worst enemy. It is shock that kills snakebite victims in the early minutes. Once you are in the hospital, you should be given antivenin and a tetanus shot, and antibiotics to prevent infection. You'll probably be out of the hospital in three days.

Don't bother to take the snake to the hospital. Most doctors can't identify it anyway. Cox says every poisonous snake has at least 18 look-alike, act-alike counterparts. Your symptoms will tell him whether you were bitten by a pit viper or coral snake, and if you received venom or not. All pit vipers have the same venom, and it is counteracted by the same antivenin.

McCook says the moccasin is one of the few snakes that will chase a person or that will let a person approach it. He believes this is not because the snake is aggressive, as many people contend, but because it is too stupid to run. He says snakes usually won't bother you, unless you bother them.

Be that as it may, last spring Milledge Sparkman and Steven Mickler were walking beside a creek before dawn during gobbler season. Mickler's pants had the seam pulled out to the knee on the left leg, and material flapped behind as he walked. Suddenly Mickler, who was in the rear, felt something caught and dragging in his torn pants leg. Thinking it was a vine, he tried several times to shake it off. Then as he took a step, it slapped the front of his right leg. Annoyed, he looked down to see the thick body of a three foot moccasin wrapping itself around his leg. To his horror, it had hung its fangs in his torn and flapping pants.

He began to jump and yell. Sparkman turned, as Mickler yelled, "Shoot it, shoot it!"

Sparkman could only respond, "I can't! I'll blow your leg off if I shoot!"

Finally, Mickler managed to step on the moccasin's tail with his right foot. He then put his left foot on the snake and worked his feet toward the snake's head. Fortunately the viper inadvertently helped by pulling back from the cloth in which its fangs were entangled, causing them to rip down the worn material a fraction of an inch from Mickler's leg. Had the snake been able to pull his fangs out of the material, he would have most surely struck again. After what seemed an eternity, his right foot was on the snake's neck and his pants leg was free.

"Get ready to shoot!" he yelled, and jumped as far as he could from the moccasin, while Sparkman blasted the venomous creature with his shotgun.

McCook may be right that a moccasin won't bother you unless you bother it. However, Mickler and Sparkman didn't intentionally bother the snake. They didn't know it was there. And had Mickler's pants legs been tight, or had he been wearing shorts as he wanted to that day (his mother persuaded the teenager not to), the snake would not have missed its target. Its fangs would have entered his leg instead of being trapped in his pants.

Experts say that most bites are caused by someone trying to pick up a snake, or by a column of people walking by it. It usually lets the first one or two pass, before it becomes annoyed or scared enough to strike

.When you visit a place where venomous snakes may be found, wear stout boots or snake leggings and loose clothing that covers your arms and legs. Look carefully before you put your hands or feet on or under limbs, logs, roots, rocks, vegetation, or on the ground, and before you sit. Never step over a log - step on top, so you can see the ground on the other side in case a snake lies there.

In the four encounters with moccasins related here, one resulted in death, one in a near fatal snake bite, one in which the intended victim was saved from snakebite by his clothing, and one in which caution prevented a moccasin bite. All of these incidents could have been fatal, but in fact, very few people die from snakebite when they receive proper medical treatment as quickly as possible. Actual data on the number of recent moccasin bites seems to be non-existent, as well as the number of resulting deaths. However, the 1983 National Center for Health Statistics lists seven fatalities nationwide from snakebite that year. And although it is estimated that Florida has approximately 100 snake bites a year, only two deaths have been reported in the last five years.

However, the cottonmouth moccasin does inflict an extremely painful and poisonous bite that can, and sometimes does, result in the loss of a limb, and less frequently, in death. So, when you visit Florida's outdoors, have fun, but be aware and be cautious. The cottonmouth lives here, and as Dan McCook says, "He's too stupid to be afraid of you."

Poisonous Mouth of the River *was not previously published, but was written in 1985. Steven is the author's son, and Milledge is a family friend. Mrs. Danese was the former Rosetta Pappy, the author's first cousin, now deceased; Euzeal Pappy, also deceased, was the author's uncle. Maynard Cox and the author became friends when she interviewed him for an article which appeared in* Fur-Fish-Game.

Maynard H. Cox, Snakebite Specialist

A tag on the front of his car says "SNAKEBITE SPECIALIST". He will remove a nuisance snake for a small fee, and he has tested snake boots for their manufacturers by allowing the snake to strike at his feet and legs while he wore them. But that's not his claim to fame. He has studied snakes for more than 48 years, and he is an expert on snakebite treatment. Maynard H. Cox is the snake man.

He is a man of average height, but that's about the only thing average about him. His hair is gray and wavy, and behind his glasses there is a twinkle in his dark brown eyes that says, "I enjoy life and I like what I do." His conversation is seasoned with wit, and he speaks faster than the southern ear is trained to hear. There isn't anything about snakes and the treatment of their bites that he doesn't know.

Cox was employed from eight to five as an Occupational Safety and Health Specialist inspector at Jacksonville, Florida Naval Air Station when we first met in the mid 1980s. He was a husband, father of six, and a grandfather. He liked to say he was also "on call 25 hours a day, eight days a week for consultation on snakebite and other poisons. I wear a beeper all the time."

Cox also lectures in seven southeastern states to audiences from kindergartners to medical personnel on snakes and other poisonous critters and the treatment of their bites and stings, as well as training emergency room personnel in the treatment of such.

He runs the World Wide Poison Bite Information Center, of which he is founder and director, out of his home in Orange Park, Florida. He obviously spends most of his at-home time in his office. When I visited his home in the 1980s, the office contained an aquarium just inside the doorway that was home to two pet red rat snakes. One was named Rosie, the snake he carried with him on the *Good Morning America Show* about that time. Bookcases overflowed with books, papers, and jars of snakes and snake eggs suspended in formaldehyde. Several large file cabinets were so full the drawers resisted closing. A large desk was piled with current work, including books from a class he was taking to help him better do his eight-to-five job.

Among the things that crowded the room were walls hung with photos of Cox with snakes; a chart of various snakes; newspaper and magazine articles about him and his work; snake skins he cured with borax, some mounted, some not; diplomas and certificates; and a poster with an excellent drawing of a rattlesnake's head, mouth open, fangs extended, that was confiscated from a college student who had advertised illegally: Wanted, Dead or Alive.

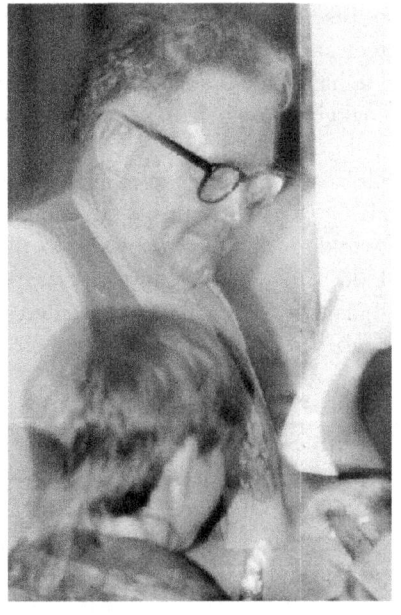

Maynard Cox lectures to boy scouts. Photo by author.

Things which had no other places were stacked on the floor among boxes as yet unpacked. There was barely room for the chairs that we sat on. This was obviously the office of an extremely busy man.

When asked how he became interested in snakes, Cox said, "I don't tell this story often, but when I was six years old I was bitten by a diamondback rattlesnake. I was living on the Nez Perces Indian Reservation in Idaho at the time. I was able to witness the sheer terror in the adults around me. I decided then and there to learn all I could about snakes. I read all the books in the school library about snakes and snakebite and memorized them all. Since then I've proven them all wrong."

Cox was born December 4, 1932, in transit back to the reservation. His family had gone to the hunting grounds and his birth was not expected until weeks later. However, on the return home a storm came and his mother went into labor. The family was forced to take shelter in a log cabin that had cracks between the logs big enough to throw things through. His father went for a midwife, but by the time he got back, Cox's grandmother had helped his mother to deliver him. The weather was -68 degrees, and the wind was blowing 60 miles per hour. The snow had drifted into 12 foot snow banks. He spent the first month of his life in the oven of a wood stove which was the only available protection from the fierce wind and cold. Cox was no more predictable when I met him than he was then, and he was just as tough. He had already survived the bites of 136 poisonous snakes by then.

Cox's father was a Nez Perces Indian, the great-grandson of Chief Joseph, the famous leader of his people who refused to give up the Wallowa Valley when his tribe was persuaded by the federal government to cede most of their lands in 1855 and 1863. After winning several battles against the army, Chief Joseph finally surrendered.

Through his father Cox had inherited Indian land and a herd of horses that was being managed by his tribe.

In 1953, Cox joined the Navy and went to Indo-China where he worked with Dr. Tom Dooley. It was Dr. Dooley who got him interested in snakebite theory and treatment. Dr. Dooley nicknamed him the snakeman, and he spoke of him in his book *Edge of Tomorrow*. Together they treated a few cobra and viper bites weekly.

Cox and Dooley wrote the forerunner to Cox's book, *Protocol for Emergency Room Procedures and Hospital Management of Snakebite* during this time.

In 1969, Cox, Dr. Newton McCullough, and the Florida State Board of Health completed research on the *McCullough Theory of Aggressive Serum Therapy for Snake Bites*.

After Cox retired from the navy he went to college and got a degree in medical lab diagnostic technology. "I married this with herpetology and found myself in a place no one had ever been before," he said.

Cox wrote his book, which he refers to as "my little red book" and opened the North Florida Snakebite treatment Center at Jacksonville, Florida Naval Air Station Hospital in 1969, using his book as a guide for treating bites. In 1973 he moved the center to Clay Memorial Hospital in Green Cove Springs, Florida, and closed it in 1985 when he reorganized as the World Wide Poison Bite and Information Center.

"I live in deadly fear I won't talk to enough people soon enough, and someone will do something dumb to himself or someone else," he said, referring to the use of snakebite kits and ice for treating bites. Snakebite kits that include devices to cut, suck, and tourniquet bites, and one to freeze bites are particular peeves of his, and he refers to them as being "as dangerous as an 'unloaded' gun." Results of the use of these kits range from loss of limb to gangrene, frostbite, and death. He has slides that show swollen, blackened, blistered and cracked flesh from the use of such devices that are horrible sights.

Cox maintains the best treatment for snakebite is to treat for shock, get the victim to a hospital immediately, and call him.

Snakebite victims who die in the first 30 minutes died from shock, not from the venom. Cox explained that shock is the result of pain and panic. The salivary glands of pit vipers (rattlesnakes, moccasins, copperheads, and pygmy rattlers) can cause an "acute inflammatory state of immunoglobulin" which burns even if it just gets on the skin and causes intense, fiery pain when injected into a victim. Add to the panic most of us have been taught to have concerning snakes and the necessary ingredients for shock are evident.

Those who die of shock are usually bitten on one of the main pipe lines of the body, according to Cox, who says these areas are the most sensitive to pain. They are: Blood artery, blood vein, lymphatic vein, and nerve trunk.

Cox had been bitten twice on a main pipeline, both by diamondbacks and each time on a finger. He said, "I'm the only human in the world, in the annals of medical history, to live through the direct intravenous injection of venom." However, rarely is one bitten on a main pipeline, he is quick to point out. It happened to him twice out of 136 bites, a percentage rate of 1.47.

Diamondback rattler. Note triangular shaped head which flares out from the body of pit vipers; photo by author.

"The only worthwhile first aid treatment is for shock. Maintain the body temperature. In shock the main organelle slows down and the body fluids don't flow. Use gravity to keep it flowing," he says. He says he once traveled for four hours in a canoe with a snake-bitten child who was in shock. He would raise the child's head when his face was pale and lower it when his face turned red. The child survived.

Since Cox maintains the venom stays in the capillary beds at the bite site, makes a wall around itself, and doesn't go anywhere for about 12 hours, if the victim doesn't die of shock, he has 12 hours to get <u>proper</u> medical care. He says most deaths and loss of limb are the result of improper medical care.

After 12 hours and the onset of the blood blisters, if a person has not received proper treatment, "The main body organs start slowing down. The weakest goes first, usually the kidneys, causing acidosis which builds up causing the lungs to quit, causing congestive heart failure and death," Cox says.

"The snake is not even immune to its own venom, and he is just as potent the day he comes out of the egg as the day he dies," he says.

The same antivenin is used for all pit vipers, and Cox says the only difference in the moccasin and the rattlesnake bite is that there are more germs in the moccasin's mouth and it sometimes carries the germ that causes gas gangrene.

Cox says don't take the snake to the hospital with you for identification. "People there are less likely than you to be able to identify it. For each poisonous snake there are at least 18 look-alike, act-alike nonpoisonous snakes," he says. Any snakebite must be treated for puncture wounds anyway, and the symptoms will tell whether or not the snake was poisonous, whether or not the snake injected venom, and if it did, what type of antivenin to administer."

Pit viper antivenin has been improved so that it rarely causes reactions. Pit vipers are milked for venom which is sent to Wyeth Laboratories where it is injected into horses. The horses' blood then makes antigen antibody complex for pit viper antivenin.

To milk the pit viper he must be forced to eject his venom into a container.

Snake bite victims are given doses of antivenin intravenously at intervals until the pain goes away. Cox's method has reduced the hospital stay to three days or less.

Approximately 10 people die annually in the US from snakebite, but about 8,000 are bitten by poisonous snakes. Cox says, "There is no reason for anyone in the United States to die of snakebite."

"The incident rate of bites is directly related to the exposure rate. There are more snake bites when school is out and people are in the woods," he says.

"When the temperature changes severely, cold nights – warm days, snakes get angry," Cox contends. They are often seen lying in the sun on logs, limbs, roads, and even in yards on such days. "Never put your hands of feet in a place you can't see," he says.

Although Cox isn't a doctor, he knows what most doctors don't about snakebites. He acts in an advisory capacity and is available for consultation 24 hours a day. He has never lost a patient or limb and had advised in the treatment of over 500 patients before I met him. He is consulted world wide.

He says, "You wouldn't go to a dentist to get eyeglasses. You shouldn't take a snake bite to someone who knows nothing about it either."

The Civil Defense Authority is so convinced Cox is the man to call for snakebite that it funds a beeper so he can be reached anytime, anyplace. And the Clay County, Florida, Sheriff's Department is so convinced that it offered the use of its phone as a community service for the same reason. Should YOU ever need the services of the snakebite specialist, dial his beeper, 904-264-6512, or for questions about snakebites, call 904-272-6398 and ask for Maynard Cox.

Anyone interested in buying a copy of Maynard Cox's book, *Protocol for Emergency Room Procedures and Hospital Management of Snakebites* can write him at 198 Venus Lane, Orange Park, Florida 32073-2431. Beyond the treatment of the above mentioned, the book tells how to identify poisonous snakes, ticks, spiders, and caterpillars.

[All of my articles about or referencing Maynard Cox are from personal interviews I conducted with him.]

The Gulf

As we sat in the lurching boat, waves breaking over the bow so high they splashed over the half top of the 19 foot craft, while lightning flashed around us, we wondered if we'd ever see the light of day.

It had started out to be a beautiful vacation. We had left Jacksonville at about 2 a.m., and after a pleasant car trip, arrived at Sugarloaf Key around noon. After unpacking our gear and having lunch, we decided to take the boat out and scout for a good place to lobster.

We had been going to the Keys in August for the past five or six years. The lobster season started then, and we all loved lobstering, fishing, swimming, snorkeling, and scuba diving. This time our vacation crew consisted of Steven, 19; Nancy, 18; Cathy, 17; Jamie, 15, Yulee, my husband; and me.

We did most of our lobstering in the Gulf of Mexico. The small channel into the Gulf from Sugarloaf Key winds through many small mangrove islands and is intersected by other small channels. All of these minor channels were poorly marked by iron pipes or wooden stakes, some of which had inverted milk jugs on top. Most of them only stuck up a foot above high tide, and many were widely space. Miles of these minor channels must be maneuvered before coming to a major channel, which is marked by the familiar red and green numbered channel markers.

Besides the difficulty of finding these small channels, there is a very real danger of running aground on grass and mud flats, or worse, putting a hole in the hull of the boat on a coral rock or one of the old, submerged pipes that previously marked the channel. Some of these are now bent from being hit by other boats, and lay in silent wait for new victims. We had experienced some of these first hand on previous vacations.

But this afternoon we had found our way out into the Gulf and to the area near Cudjoe Key with no problems. This had been a productive place on previous vacations. The skies were clear and a light breeze blew, making the steamy weather more comfortable; the kids made a few dives, catching six or seven good-size lobsters.

About 5 P.M., Yulee decided we'd better head back to Sugarloaf. We'd all been up since before 2 a.m., with only three or four hours sleep before that. Everyone began to think with longing of the steaks I had put on the kitchenette drain board to thaw for supper at the lodge, too.

We got about halfway in when a dark storm cloud suddenly appeared ahead. As the cloud moved closer and visibility diminished, it became harder to see the channel markers. To make matters worse, white birds on mud flats were confusing us. We kept mistaking them for the milk jugs on pipes that marked much of the channel. We repeatedly ran onto the flats and had to use precious time getting the boat back into the channel, which was as narrow as five feet in many places.

When skies are clear, it's daylight until about 9 p.m. in the Keys in August; by 7 o'clock this particular evening, it was dark. We were in a basin surrounded by several tiny mangrove islands, as the wind began to blow. Then the dark clouds overhead burst with blinding lighting and simultaneous, nerve-jangling thunder. Pelting rain stung us as we were suddenly drenched in spite of the boat's fiberglass half-top. We pulled the life vests from their storage in the bow and put them on. It was looking increasingly threatening.

Yulee knew we were very close to Sugarloaf Key, but he couldn't take a chance on running aground or onto a coral reef in the worsening storm. He decided to wait out the storm because of the impossibility of navigation in such conditions. But each time he put the anchor out, the rough sea and wind pulled it loose.

Finally, because of the shallow basin we were in and the huge coral heads which could tear the bottom out of the boat, Yulee shouted over the sounds of the storm, "I'll have to jump over and hook the anchor in a coral rock."

"No,!" we all screamed together, as our boat bobbed in the churning water. You can't get out in that water! You might step in a hole. Lightning might strike you. You might lose the boat in the darkness and waves," we protested in terror. But even as we tried to dissuade him, the anchor came loose again, bringing the bow against a coral head and throwing us off our seats.

Yulee found the flashlight and handed it to Steven. "Hold this on the anchor," he said, as he opened the windshield and began to crawl over the bucking bow toward where the anchor line was tied. Taking a firm hold of the line, he let himself into the water as carefully as he could.

Fighting the wind and waves, he finally got the anchor secured after several attempts, while his family watched in terror and silently prayed. He pulled his way back to the boat with the help of the anchor rope which he had never let go of, and Steven helped him back into the boat. He crouched, shivering as seaweed fell from his arms and legs. Then I remembered putting six nylon wind breakers into a canvas tote under one of the seats. The girls and I shielded the tote from the rain with our bodies as I opened it, and pulled out two towels there also. Everything else was dripping wet. I wrapped one of the towels around Yulee's shoulders, alarmed at the blue goose-pimply appearance of his skin in the brief but numerous flashes of light. We all dried off as best we could and got into the wind breakers; we were soaked again in seconds. The boat had no cover for the sides or back, only the top front. Water and wind forced their way between the windshield and the top in front, so there was no dry place. Although the Keys are usually sweltering in August, we were all cold and shivering.

Meanwhile, the storm raged on. We realized we were in a very dangerous situation. At any minute the wind and waves could capsize the boat or lightning could strike it. And I tried not to remember the funnel of water we had witnessed in the Gulf a mile or so away one clear day last summer. It had moved lazily along, like a curved finger of water spiraling upward into an otherwise undisturbed sky. What if this storm spawned a waterspout or tornado?

My children made me very proud, because no one panicked, although there were occasional comments about being cold, hungry, and something smelling awful. Although no one got seasick a terrible odor in the boat made us all nauseous and gave us headaches. We decided the odor came from the life vests, but we dared not take them off.

Jamie was the first to fall asleep; he had curled up on the floor beneath the dash. Steven and Cathy fell asleep a little later. I couldn't believe they could sleep with waves crashing over the top of the boat which was being tossed about on the angry sea, as lightning cracked and sizzled all around us, but I was thankful they could. We had all been up more than 20 hours, and we were bone tired, but Nancy, Yulee and I couldn't sleep.

I am the cold natured one in the family, and although I was chilled, I was alarmed at the shivering and teeth-chattering that my husband was experiencing. I rubbed his arms and put both soaking towels around him. Every 30 minutes or so, he would bail water out of the engine compartment. He had decided when the storm began not to use the bulge pump in order to conserve the battery.

Once while he was bailing water, he was thrown against the side of the boat with such force he would have fallen overboard if a sudden wave hadn't tilted the boat in the other direction at just the right moment.

Finally, after about seven hours of ferocious winds, pelting rain, threatening lightning, and seas with waves that crashed over and into the boat, the storm abated as abruptly as it had begun. As the clouds moved on, the moon appeared as though smiling in apology at the antics of the fickle weather of summer.

Yulee pointed to something that was revealed in the moonlight. It was a huge crane that sat by the highway where a new bridge was being constructed near Sugarloaf Lodge. We were within 20 minutes of our warm, dry beds and a hot meal, but we knew we couldn't make our way through the treacherous rocks and flats until full daylight.

We had nearly four hours before daylight, but we knew we were going to make it! We had escaped the twin clutches of King Neptune and Mother Nature, and even though we had felt terror at times and had been miserable all night, we suffered no permanent damage. We said a prayer of thanks.

With the arrival of dawn, Steven, Cathy, and Jamie woke up. Yulee bailed the engine compartment out one last time. Everyone commented on the awful, nauseating odor once more. As we tidied up the boat and wrung water out of towels and jackets, Nancy noticed the seaweed that had fallen off Yulee when he climbed back into the boat after setting the anchor the night before. When she picked it up, she exclaimed, "Yuk! This stuff stinks! This is what's been making us sick." She was right. After she threw it back into the sea the odor disappeared, and we began to feel better.

Miraculously, the boat started, and within a few minutes Yulee had found the channel. We were back at the lodge within half an hour. No one can imagine the thrill of getting his feet on solid ground again after such an ordeal unless it has happened to him.

Nancy Mickler holding lobsters she caught. Photo by author.

We were ravenous, and of course, the steaks were spoiled. After a huge breakfast of bacon and eggs, we went to bed at 8 a.m. Yulee, Nancy and I had been awake for more than 30 hours! Bed had never felt so good before, and we slept 'til three in the afternoon.

The following day we were out in the Gulf again, but were careful to start back in by 4 p.m. We were also careful to check the weather forecast before we got in the boat.

The rest of our vacation was great, and we got our limit of lobsters most days, but none of us will ever forget the stormy night we spent with some nauseating seaweed in a bucking 19-foot boat in the shallow, angry water of the Gulf of Mexico.

The Gulf *was first published in* Florida Living, *November 1986, North Florida Publishing Company, Inc., 102 N. E. 10th Avenue, Gainesville, Florida 32601, pages 42, 43.*

Call of the Gobbler

The man could barely drag himself to his car. His wife accompanied him, because she was afraid for him to go alone. Although he insisted on driving, she had to open the door for him to get in the car, and again for him when he got out.

He had been injured at work two days earlier when a ton and a half of conveyor chain had broken and fallen on him, causing contusions and lacerations all over his body, and a broken rib. According to doctors, every bone in his body should be broken, and he was lucky to be alive. He was extremely stiff and in great pain.

Still, he had a week off to recuperate, and it was gobbler season. The man belonged to a peculiar breed: he was a turkey hunter. The call of the gobbler beckoned, and nothing short of a body cast could keep him out of the woods.

When they arrived at his destination, his wife helped him out of the car, shouldered his shotgun, tested the depth of the water in the ditch, so he wouldn't get his feet wet (or step in a hole and fall), and put up a camouflage net. Then he set to work with his mouth yelper. There was no immediate resounding gobble, but the man knew a huge gobbler frequented the area. A few days earlier he had seen the old tom's tracks and the scratches from his wing tips where he had been strutting up and down the white sand road for 300 yards. And judging from the hen tracks, his harem must number at least 10 hens. Anyway, the gobblers hadn't been too vocal this season, and he wasn't going to give up.

About 8 a.m., the man stretched out on the ground trying to get more comfortable. He ached all over and felt weak and dizzy. He still hadn't seen or heard anything. He changed callers, thinking a new voice might entice a gobbler to answer or to come in silently.

Finally, about 10 a.m., his wife heard a gobble. She tried to get his attention. He was about 20 feet away and looking in the opposite direction. A few minutes later she heard it a second time. At about that time her husband looked at her and said, "Let's go." She signaled to him she had heard a turkey gobble. In a minute, the old tom gobbled again, closer and louder, and he heard it too.

He laid his gun beside him, and soon they could see the blue-white head through the bushes as the gobbler came down the road. Its tail feathers were spread, breast feathers fluffed, folded skin on its neck bright red, and it was leisurely strutting toward them, arrogantly tilting its head as though it were king of the forest. The morning sun sparkled on its wings and spread fan reflecting bronze, emerald, ruby and sapphire - jeweled colors that seemed to confirm his royalty. He was indeed a majestic bird; his beard was so long he nearly walked on it, and his long, sharp spurs were undoubtedly capable of inflicting great pain on any rival for the affection of his harem.

This magnificent bird stepped into a clearing about 25 feet in front of the couple, an awesome sight in search of his lovelorn queen. He paused and tilted his head questionably.

The magnificent gobbler; photo by author.

The wife whispered, "Shoot him," and was amazed to see her husband hadn't even picked up his gun.

King gobbler continued to dazzle them with his displayed finery for a few more seconds, turned and nonchalantly pranced unhurriedly back in the direction from which he had come, no doubt confident his loud, and unseen, queen would follow

As the big gobbler disappeared behind the underbrush, the lady asked, "Why didn't you shoot it?"

The turkey hunter answered, "I thought of how my shoulder is black and blue, my ribs are broken, and I hurt all over. I remembered how my 12 gauge kicks. I thought of the excitement and beauty of what just happened; and I knew if I shot, it would just hurt me so badly I wouldn't be able to get out of bed and come back tomorrow.

I can testify that this story is true, because I was the only witness to this lapse into insanity. For a second I even thought my husband had suddenly reverted to the normal, sane person he really is, that he had realized he should be home watching TV or reading a book. Then he had given his reason for not shooting - he wanted to come back tomorrow! I knew right then and there that people who belong to this particular breed lose their sanity when the moon rises on the eve of gobbler season, and they don't completely return to normal until the sun sets on the last day of it.

Call of the Gobbler *was first published in* Turkey, *September 1984, Pages 28, 48, Spearman Publishing and Printing, Inc., 213 North Saunders, Sutton, NE 68979.*

Why Not Bring *Two Loves* Together?

In Jacksonville, Florida, there is a very intelligent man who is not only an excellent turkey hunter, but a very good amateur psychologist, also. This man realized he had a happy marriage, and he wanted to keep it that way, but one Friday night during spring gobbler season, as he was preparing his gear for a Saturday morning turkey hunt, his wife said, "You're not going to turkey hunt again tomorrow, are you? We haven't spent a Saturday or Sunday together since the season started."

Realizing one of the loves of his life was about to come between himself and the other love of his life, he did some quick thinking. He knew she was a crack shot, but she'd never hunted anything except squirrels. Still, she liked the woods, and she was a good sport. Why not bring his two loves together? This turkey hunter turned psychologist said, "Honey, I have a great idea. I know where there is an old gobbler. Come with me tomorrow, and I'll call him to you."

Now, this shrewd fellow knew something his wife didn't; turkey hunting is addictive. He thoroughly intended to give his wife the habit. He knew that all he had to do was get her to hear that old gobbler and get a glimpse of it, and she'd be hooked. It wouldn't even be necessary for her to get a shot at it, let alone get her hand around its neck. Hadn't her dad hooked him on the sport in exactly the same way?

She finally agreed to go, but stipulated that on Sunday he had to go to a family reunion with her. He grinned to himself, this sly fellow, because if all went as planned, he was going to get out of that reunion – and what's more, she would suggest it.

The clock rang at 4:00 a.m. the next morning. He gently nudged his wife and said, "Honey, time to get up." This proved to be the hardest part, because his wife was something of a sleepy-head; 4:00 a.m., to her, was the middle of the night. After re-convincing her (he could already see an unhappy future if he didn't get her as excited about turkey hunting as he was), they dressed quickly, fixed fried egg sandwiches and a thermos of coffee which they had on the road, and headed for the spot where the old gobbler waited (he hoped and prayed) to help him institute his devious plan.

They arrived at their destination well before 6:00 a.m. He pulled off the road, got out and hooted like an owl. Immediately the cooperative gobbler split the silence with an eerie gobble. She asked, "What's that?"

He explained that was a gobbler, and she'd best hurry, because they had to get in the woods, build a blind and be hidden before daylight, which was minutes away.

He led her down a fire trail toward the swamp. Then he began to search for a place to set up a blind, whispering to her that the ideal spot would have two large trees which they could put their backs up against, both to protect them from the shots of other hunters and for comfort. It would also have at least a 180 degree view. In a little while, he found what he called "the perfect spot." He told her to sit down in front of the tree that was slightly in front and to the right of the other, put her gun (she carried a Remington 20 gauge pump) to her shoulder, and move it in arc. Then he cut down all the bushes and grasses the barrel touched. He explained this was to prevent movement and noise from attracting the turkey's ever-vigilant eye. Next, he cut some palmettos and stuck them in the ground in front and on both sides to hide them from the turkey. Now he was ready to sit down in front of the other tree to wait until daylight when he would make his first call.

His caller was an old corncob striker and an oval piece of slate made for him by her dad. Just after daylight he used it to make a series of three calls, and the gobbler barely waited for him to finish before it answered. This time, his wife recognized the sound, and just as he knew it would, her adrenalin began to flow. Expectation and excitement united; her heart began to pound so loudly that she was afraid the turkey would hear it and be scared away.

Just as she began to feel normal again, her husband played another tune with his striker, and the gobbler answered immediately as before. He knew the love-starved gobbler could fly down at any minute. She was having trouble keeping her knees from knocking, so excited was she. She just knew the turkey would appear any minute, and she had him counted!

It was another 45 minutes before they heard the great wings of the big gobbler flapping as it left the limb. The man recognized the sound, but it startled his wife. However, she had been warned not to talk, so she couldn't ask what made the noise.

The next time the man called, the gobbler's answer came from the left and farther away. She thought it was leaving, and her heart sank. But her husband didn't give up. He couldn't – too much was at stake. He had heard a hen call in the direction the gobbler was headed. He either had to call the gobbler away from the hen, or hope the gobbler would come to his call after taking care of the unwelcome intruder.

For a while the turkey's gobble alternated between being closer to the hunters and closer to the hen. The excitement and disappointment were getting to be too much for her to bear. Then, suddenly, it seemed like nothing but a palmetto patch separated them from the gobbler. It would gobble; then there would be a strange thump-thump sound; and then a sound like something sweeping the pine straw and leaves that littered the ground. Although she didn't recognize this sound either, he knew the gobbler was strutting.

Eventually, she saw a blue head come out from behind the palmettos and pull back, then the spread fan of the turkey's tail. She was fascinated, excited, and unable to move. She had heard her dad talk about what he called the "heebie geebies," and she realized this was what she was experiencing.

After about five minutes of this courting ritual in which she occasionally saw the turkey's head and then his tail feathers, another turkey appeared. It came from the right and disappeared behind the palmettos with the gobbler. Other strange noises were heard, then silence. A hen had come up and stolen her excited gobbler, calmed it down, and walked off with it!

All the time, her husband sat behind her; it was all he could do to keep from laughing. He knew he could have killed the gobbler, but he also knew she was getting the fever. From now on she would be as avid a turkey hunter as he. He was both amused by what had taken place, and excited that his plan had worked. He had also relived the excitement of his first encounter with an old gobbler several years earlier when her father had been in his place, and he had in hers. He innocently asked her, "Why didn't you shoot it?"

She answered, "I thought it would come out of the palmettos where I'd get a better shot. Was that a hen that enticed MY turkey away?"

He told her that it was, and that it was all over for today. She said, "Can we come back tomorrow and try again?"

Answering with tongue in cheek, he said, "Sorry, honey, we have to go to that family reunion tomorrow."

She replied, "Oh, come on. You know you were only going to please me." He "reluctantly" let her talk him out of the family reunion.

Author with her first turkey, abt. 1977; photo by Yulee Mickler.

The next morning she was awake when the clock went off. This time the gobbler came to her husband's call and brought the hen with him. This time he didn't stay behind the palmettos. And this time, in spite of the "heebie geebies", she shot her gobbler in the head and neck with a load of high brass 7 ½ shot. It weighed 16 pounds and had a 9 ¾ inch beard, which is a nice size for a Florida gobbler; in these parts the rarely weigh more than 18 pounds.

His psychology had worked just as he had planned. He has gotten her addicted to his habit. This happened about eight years ago, and their marriage has remained happy. They still hunt turkeys together in the woods of Northeast Florida, but more often than not, she carries a camera instead of a gun, and now believes it's harder to get a turkey on film than into the pan. Just in case you wondered, the sly turkey hunter who succeeded in bringing his two loves together is Yulee Mickler, and I am the other love in his life.

Why Not Bring Two Loves Together? *was first published in* Turkey – Monthly Magazine for Turkey Hunters, Vol. 2, No.1, March 1985.

Tom Meets the Temptress

She was full-bodied and beautiful, and she had lain on the closet shelf in her mesh bag for over a year. She had not been called upon before because in the areas I had hunted, the toms were under intense hunting pressure and it may have been dangerous for the temptress, not to mention me.

This gobbler season, though, I had hunted an area for four days where the toms were vocal and I hadn't seen or heard another hunter. I decided to call the temptress into service to help lure a certain tom I had talked to each morning. I was determined to at least see him.

Yulee had a week of vacation and we had taken our newly acquired secondhand motor home to a campground near Ocala, Florida, where we belong to a hunting club, for a full week of chasing spring gobblers. I had hunted with Yulee a day here and weekend there, but with running a home for eight people, I was never able to go for more than two days in a row. This week it was just Yulee and me, and I had no other duty than to cook for the two of us. In those seven days I learned more than in all the years of hunting a day now and then. These lessons included patience, perseverance, and ignoring a bottom that is sore from hours of sitting on a cold, damp seat. Why, you might ask, did I subject myself to such misery? Well, if you ask that, you are not a turkey hunter. Any turkey hunter will tell you the sport is addictive.

The first morning I heard four gobblers. All of them answered the lonesome calls I made on the box, but none came. The second day Yulee was hunting about a mile away and called and killed a 16 $\frac{1}{4}$ pound gobbler with an 8 $\frac{1}{4}$ inch beard. Although two had answered my seductive calls, they had not come and all was quiet after 6:30 a.m.

Tuesday one of the two toms that had been taunting me came closer, passing on my right too far away to be seen through the underbrush. All was quiet except for my own calls until about 8:30 when a turkey gobbled on my right. Each time I yelped, his answering gobble was closer until he was only about 100 yards away. Around nine, Yulee walked up whistling to let me know he was there. He scared a hen that was probably hoping I would call a tom to her. She jumped into my blind in a palmetto patch, ran several wild circles, and flew as far away as she could fly. The gobbling was over for the morning.

**Yulee's gobbler.
Photo by author.**

That afternoon, we moved my blind down the swamp a few hundred yards to the right, and on the fourth day the nearest of the answering gobblers came closer, again going by on the right. A hen in the palmettos yelped as she passed behind me to rendezvous with the old rake. I had wondered why he didn't come to me. At eleven I gave up. The tom hadn't gobbled in my hearing since 6:30. That's when I decided to call on the temptress. I had the swamp to myself, so I figured we'd be safe. To be sure, we carried her in the woods that afternoon and chose a place to put her stake in the ground where a tree would block me from any shots fired in my direction by a misguided hunter that missed her.

Thursday morning was a replay of Wednesday until 6:30 with the hen again leaving me to intercept the old guy and traipsing off with him while I sat alone. Although lots of hunters go to gobblers, I don't. I like the challenge of making them come to me, and unfortunately, I get turned around easily. Being lost, I had discovered long ago, was no fun.

I continued to yelp every ten minutes even after the gobbling stopped. At ten I was rewarded with a gobble on my right. After sounding off four times, each closer than the last, he hushed, even though I waited another hour before leaving.

By then I was pretty frustrated. I only had two more days, and I had fooled with this guy all week. He still hadn't even had a look at the temptress. But he did get closer each day. With the eternal hope of a turkey hunter, I though *maybe tomorrow*.

Friday the tom passed even closer, and the hen yelped an invitation for me to join her as she took her usual stroll to meet him. Then, at 7:30, I heard leaves rustle to my right. Peering through the palmettos, my eyes met those of a jake not 10 feet away. My heart thumped hard and loud. I just knew he'd seen me when he turned his head and his eyes beheld the temptress about 30 feet away. He ran straight to her, purring all the way. Standing on the other side of the alluring lady, he put his beak to her ear and he purred – and he purred – and he purred. I had gotten my 20 gauge Ithaca pump on him when he had gone behind a tree. By now my arm was shaking from holding the normally lightweight gun. I felt like a peeping tom, but I wanted to see what the jake would do. He seemed bent on sweet-talk all day.

If I didn't shoot him soon, I'd have to put the gun down. In any case, the show would be over because at such a short distance, his sharp eyes would have seen any movement. He wouldn't come from behind the temptress, but I knew she was made of tough stuff, and few shot wouldn't hurt too much. I didn't realize how badly my arm was shaking, and when I pulled the trigger, the whole load hit the temptress in the side. She turned on her stake, and her tail slapped the jake – hard. He went off rather fast in the direction from whence he had come, looking over his shoulder with a broken-hearted expression on his once ecstatic face. I hope I didn't cause the young fellow to give up on romance.

The jake wasn't the big boy I had heard gobble every morning, though. I hoped his curiosity would bring him close enough to meet the temptress Saturday, my last day. I couldn't wait.

Next morning the boss gobbled at 6:10, so far away I wasn't sure it was a gobble. I answered and when he next gobbled, he had closed the distance some. By 6:20, he was just out of sight behind the thick undergrowth 100 feet away. Every few minutes he gobbled. Sometimes I'd softly yelp or cluck, bringing an immediate excited gobble. He didn't shut up when I was silent, though. He was on fire from the promised rapture of a week's worth of sweet talk. After about 30 minutes, his head and chest appeared above the bushes. Then he stepped into full view, his head red, white, and blue; wattles engorged with blood; five inch snood draped over his beak; feathers on end and reflecting rainbow colors in the morning sun.

His wing tips dragged the ground and his thick, black beard divided a puffed-up chest. He pranced slowly across the area between the thick undergrowth and me, his eyes on the place his keen ears told him the promises emanated from. Only scattered palms and cypresses were between him and the temptress. About 75 feet from me he disappeared behind a cypress, and I got the gun up. When he finally reappeared, he had seen the hen. His pace quickened, his step became jauntier. No doubt his heart beat faster, too, as mine did. He was totally smitten. All was silent as he strutted and pranced and displayed while covering the last 50 feet.

When he approached her side, he strutted all the way around her, his face always to her. I saw the magnificent old tom in full strut from every direction as he looked her over from all angles. When at last he stood face-to-face with her, he was still except for an occasional convulsive quivering downward of his wings.

My gun was getting heavy as I held it on his head. Still, watching the two finally facing each other as he stared at her intently, I HAD to see what the cock-of-the-woods would do after meeting the temptress.

Well, the old boy got pretty irritated at this tease that he thought had promised him everything for a whole week, and now that he stood a foot away, she only tried to outstare him. Exasperated, he suddenly lifted his right wing and slapped her face quick and hard. She turned halfway around on her stake, and I decided it was time to shoot. The temptress had been treated badly enough these last two days – shot yesterday, slapped today – besides, this old boy had been around a long time. I knew it would be but a split second before he decided the temptress was a dummy. Remembering my shaky arm yesterday, I willed it still and gently squeezed the trigger. The knees buckled on 16 ½ pounds of Tom Turkey at 6:58 a.m. Meeting the temptress had been Tom's final and fatal mistake.

Tom turkey and me; photo by author's husband Yulee.

The gobbler had an 8 ½ inch beard and 1 ¼ inch spurs. Two deep and recent spur wounds scarred his chest. [Could he have gotten those while trying to get to my seductive call earlier this week:?] He had given me an exciting week with a perfect ending and taught me that anticipation and a week of working a bird make eventual success more rewarding.

Tom Turkey Meets the Temptress *was previously published in* Turkey, Monthly Magazine for Turkey Hunters, Vol. 2, No. 10, December 1985.

How to Count Turkeys

"Prrt!" The sound was loud and to my left. Powerful wings flapped and over a fallen tree forty feet away two turkeys jumped into the air slapping at each other. Under an arch in the downed tree another turkey was rolling end over end. The third turkey regained his feet and jumped back into the melee, while over the top of the fallen tree another turkey head appeared momentarily as it nonchalantly ate the flowers from a jasmine vine. To the right of these four, I could see the legs of a fifth turkey.

It was opening morning of the spring season, and it was looking good. I had followed a familiar path to the edge of a Florida swamp. I had started to the right when a herd of deer raced through the mud and water near me, disturbing the quiet. A sudden gobble shook the very air. The originator of the eerie sound that is music to a turkey hunter's ears was in a tree which I would have passed under. As I froze in my tracks and the deer continued on, the bird gobbled three times. My mouth curled into an involuntary smile.

He's here, I thought, *and the deer kept me from walking under his tree and scaring him off.*

I went to the left about a hundred yards away, the old bird thundering off constantly. There wasn't time to make a blind and nothing to make one with. I sat between the roots of a large tree facing the swamp, the gun across my legs. I pulled my hat down to the top of my glasses and my net mask up to the bottom of them. After pulling on my gloves, I pulled a box call from my bag and made a tree yelp.

"Gobble-obble-obble!" came the excited answer.

A few minutes later the bird gobbled again, and he was coming. Within ten minutes that turkey was marching back and forth in front of me in the swamp, gobbling constantly, but I couldn't see him.

After 30 minutes and still no sight of him, something iridescent glinted in the early morning light. Looking closely I saw something blue and shiny and low to the ground. I watched it for about 10 minutes before a slight movement confirmed my suspicions: there was another gobbler even closer than the loud mouth.

Before I could lift my gun the closer turkey stood up and walked to within twelve feet of me, looking straight at me.

Just then the other gobbler stepped into view in the swamp. I could tell he was the boss. He was the biggest turkey I had seen, and he was out of gunshot range. His head was bright red, and when he gobbled the nearer bird made a beeline for the boss. I could have killed him then, but I was picky. I wanted the monster I had talked to all morning.

He went to the gobbling turkey and walked along side as the boss strutted and gobbled. The second bird never lifted his feathers or opened his mouth. This went on for another 30 minutes. Each time the old bird gobbled, they would both stop, look in my direction and stretch their necks to the limit. They appeared to almost stand on tiptoe in their attempts to see the hen they knew was there. Any sound from my call brought a double or triple gobble. But the turkeys wouldn't leave the strutting ground.

Finally all gobbling ceased, and I could see neither bird. I thought they had given up on the invisible hen. About ten minutes later I heard a loud Prrrt, to my left.

I could see the heads of the three I knew were male when they jumped up to slap or spur each other. I decided I was going to shoot the next time one of them jumped up to show me his head. I got the gun up, safety off, and didn't have long to wait. The turkey that appeared seemed to have been thrown into the air. I shot. The rest ran or flew off.

When I retrieved my bird, it wasn't either of the big guys, but it was a nice jake. I left the woods about 8 o'clock.

I had to wait for Yulee to pick me up as he had the truck. By 8:30 the gobbler was back there. I heard him gobbling in the same place. When Yulee walked up the old guy opened his mouth again.

I told Yulee my story, and said, "Why don't you try him? He's the biggest turkey I ever saw."

Yulee said, "No, you come back and try him again tomorrow."

I had never killed my limit (two per season) in the first two days, but I really thought I would this year. Mentally, I counted number two.

Next day my daughter, home from college on spring break, wanted to go with me. Nancy is a marine biology student and loves to observe nature.

I led her to within 25 feet of where the boss had strutted the previous day. When I gave my tree yelp, a gobble came right back. As before, he came to strut out of sight and gunshot. Suddenly a low yelp sounded form the left, and I saw a second gobbler closer. I knew Nancy, who'd never seen a turkey strut or a gobbler up close, could not see him from where she sat. I decided to try to get him closer.

I could still hear the other turkey gobbling, but he wasn't coming closer. I decided I'd kill this one if I could after Nancy saw him, because the boss evidently didn't go to his hens. The closer turkey yelped. I yelped. He purred. I purred. Every sound he made, I made. But he kept a large tree between himself and me. The tree was about five feet from me and slightly to my left. I tried to look around first one side, then the other. Nancy, who was about six feet behind and to my right, finally whispered, "Close and to your right."

Just as I leaned to the right with my shotgun up and ready, he stepped into view. The boss gobbler gobbled in the distance. But this one was in my gun sight. He appeared to be the same turkey that had come so close yesterday. At least he was about the same size with a similar beard. I pulled the trigger. "Pffft," the gun said, and I heard

BB's hit the palmetto blind in front of me. The turkey disappeared behind the tree again and flew off.

"What happened?" asked Nancy. "He should be dead" He was so close: The gun hardly made a sound!"

"I don't know," I said. "I thought he was mine." Then I remembered something my Daddy said.

"Do you know how to count turkeys? When you shoot him, you go to him, lean down and put your hand around his neck, and you say 'one'."

Later Yulee told me the shell had obviously gotten wet. The inside of the gun barrel was covered with wet gunpowder, and the wadding from the shell was still in the gun. If I had gotten a second shot, I probably would have warped the barrel when the next shell hit that wadding.

I didn't get my limit in two days, but Nancy and I had an exciting morning. She got to see a gobbler up close, even though he didn't strut. We heard the boss gobble. On the way out of the woods the old red-head ran across our path and she caught a glimpse of the boss.

Next weekend I was back with no luck. On the way out of the woods Yulee told me he had talked to another hunter that morning. He said that on the third day of the season (the day after Nancy and I had been there) he'd killed a 22 pound gobbler right where I had been. He'd been unable to call him close and had shot him with a rifle at a long distance.

"I told you he was the biggest turkey I'd ever seen," I told Yulee. And I was more than a little upset that I couldn't count him. Twenty-two pounds is a real trophy for an Osceola gobbler. Fifteen or sixteen pounds is about average.

Given the unpredictable nature of the turkey (which is really the only predictable thing about the creatures), Daddy was right. Don't count your turkey until you get your hand around his feet of neck. Enjoy the hunt, but don't EXPECT to kill a turkey. The pleasure and excitement of the hunt is a reward in itself. Getting a turkey is only an occasional bonus.

(How to Count Turkeys *was previously published in* The Turkey Hunter, *Vol. 6, No. 5, August/September, 1989.*)

Believe it or *Not!*

"Flip, Flip, Flip," the sound was unmistakable.

"A turkey just flew," said Yulee.

"Didn't sound like it went far," I said.

We were walking in a Florida swamp looking for turkey sign and a place to build a blind so I could photograph the turkeys we knew were in the area. The day was cool and windy, a February afternoon a little past five. The caretaker of the property, Beverly Fleming, had been letting me attempt to photograph the turkeys; we had already heard turkey gobbling and seen them strutting near here.

Walking a little farther, we again heard the sound of turkey wings. Yulee Said, "That turkey's on the ground. It must be hurt, or something has caught it."

A few steps farther and we both saw the turkey, a hen. "She's in the water," I said.

Yulee walked toward the turkey which was frantically flapping its wing to no avail.

"She won't last the night. A wildcat or coon or something will get her. I'll see if I can get her loose and see how bad she's hurt," Yulee said.

He felt around in the water with his hand. He had one arm wrapped around the hen holding her to his body to stop the wing-beating and to prevent his being clawed by the free foot. With the other hand he held the trapped leg. "I'll have to pick her up higher to see what's holding her."

But she was held fast and he didn't pull her far for fear of hurting her worse. "There's something big and round here. I think it's a turtle." He was probing with his feet. "I'll have to pull her up to see how bad it's got her." As he pulled, the head of an alligator turtle appeared, and the middle toe of the hen's foot was in its mouth to about an inch from the pad of her foot! The toe was all but severed.

For those unfamiliar with alligator turtles, let me tell you they are something you don't want to get tangled up with. They have heads and tails similar to alligators, and they are more than eager to use their most vicious part, which in this instance, held a small turkey toe. At any second this prehistoric-appearing creature could release the turkey toe for a human hand or foot.

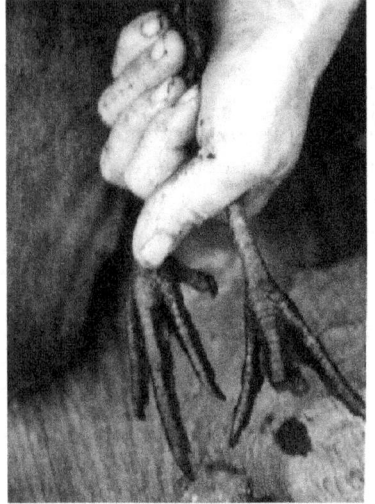

Yulee holds turkey's feet after releasing it from turtle; photo by author.

"Come hold the turkey like this:, he held her out to me by the wings where they joined the body . "I'll have to cut the skin this toe is hanging by, to get her free of the turtle. There's no way we'll get the rest of the toe out of the turtle's mouth. Anyway, it's barely hanging and would have to come off," Yulee said.

I don't mind telling you I was reluctant to get so close to a creature I knew to be so vicious, and I didn't like the idea of my husband's hand being where the turkey's toe now was, either. However, the look I got from Yulee left me no choice.

After freeing the bird from the turtle, he said, "Now what are we going to do with her? That toe is bleeding badly. If I let her go, something will catch her. It's already after fly-up time and getting too dark for a turkey to see much."

"She's wet and shivering. Look at her breast feathers. A lot of them are gone. She appears to be in shock. Let's take her to Beverly; she sometimes nurses sick or hurt birds and animals. Maybe she can keep it till it's well, then let it go near the rest of the flock," I said. The mating season was about to start, so this hen could lay and hatch a clutch of eggs if she survived.

The hen seemed to cuddle up to the warmth of Yulee's body as he carried her out of the swamp. In the Jeep she lay on the seat without attempting to move. I just put my hand around her legs, and she didn't even struggle.

Beverly was astounded by the story we had to tell her. She taped the turkey's legs together gently and wrapped it in a towel. She then put a piece of tape around it to immobilize the bird and keep it warm. When her husband came home a few minutes later, they took the turkey to a veterinarian.

Dr. Jeffrey Woods took the bone out of the remaining piece of toe to the pad of the foot, sewed the skin over the wound, and gave the hen antibiotics. Next day Beverly went to St. Augustine to meet with officials of the Wildlife Rehabilitation Center. They gave her permission to keep the turkey until it could be released.

The hen broke part of her beak that day trying to peck her way out, so she had to be hooded to prevent her from injuring herself. She was kept in the bathtub and allowed to walk a little in the kitchen. By the second day she was standing a little on the injured foot. She had to be hand fed because the hood had to stay on to prevent her hurting herself.

Dr. Woods came to Beverly's a few days later, bringing officials from the local college. Some had never seen a wild turkey before. They were so intrigued, the head of the science department wanted to try to videotape the flock for use in the school's science class. (I can tell him from experience it won't be easy.)

The hen recovered even after getting an infection in her foot and was released to the flock a few weeks later.

Although hunting is allowed on some parts of this property, it isn't where we found the hen or near Beverly's home.

Are we hunters: You bet! You might wonder why, then, this turkey's life was important to us when hunters kill turkeys. Well, if turkey hunters are not conservationists, if we do not protect the birds we harvest, turkey hunting will face a bleak future. It wasn't hunting season, and this was a hen. One hen can hatch as many as 17 eggs, according to wild turkey experts. The next season the hens from this hatching that survive may do the same, and on and on. One hen could be responsible for more than all the turkeys a hunter can legally take in his lifetime.

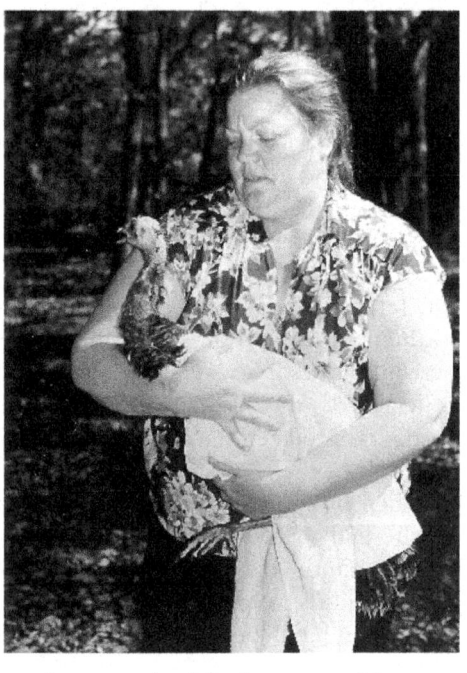

Bev Fleming prepares to release hen; photo by author.

I knew that turtles catch ducks, but somehow a turtle as a turkey predator never entered my mind. I certainly had never heard of it before, nor has anyone I've discussed it with. If we hadn't been looking for a place to build a photography blind, we would never have seen it, and without evidence, I'm not sure I would believe it if I had been told.

Who would ever have thought a turtle could catch a turkey? Yulee and I saw it with our own eyes, and you can believe it or not.

Believe it or Not *was first published in* The Turkey Hunter, *Vol. 8, No. 7, October/November 1991.*

Acknowledgments

A special thanks is due to my neighbors and friends, R. J. and Juanita Wilson for their help with the lead story in this book. They answered questions and volunteered vital information about Sampson, the surrounding area, and some of the former residents.

R. J. told me about his experiences as a young boy in the cattle business as well as stories about his family in Sampson. In addition, they allowed me the use of R. J.'s deceased mother Eva Foster Wilson's scrapbooks and photograph albums. They even spent an afternoon riding me around and refreshing my memory on the location of some of the old places remembered from my childhood and showing me some that I didn't remember. Most of these places are now inaccessible or are obliterated and forgotten due to pine plantations or to housing developments built on top of them.

As always when it comes to computer projects, I must thank my daughter Cathy Ammons who is the computer expert in the family. She always made herself available for any help I needed in this department, whether the problem was technical or because of my ineptitude.

Thank you R. J., Juanita, and Cathy. I love you all.

Latrell Pappy Mickler
Sampson, Florida
June 20, 2009

Made in the USA
Columbia, SC
27 May 2018